It is indeed wonderful to think how very different is the England in which we live to-day, from that in which we might possibly have been living were it not for the great and famous engineer George Stephenson.

This book is dedicated to

GEORGE STEPHENSON 1781–1848 – "FATHER OF THE RAILWAYS"

ALKEN'S ILLUSTRATION OF MODERN PROPHECY

REGENT'S PARK - 1831

ALKEN'S ILLUSTRATION OF MODERN PROPHECY

WHITE CHAPEL ROAD - 1830

NORTHUMBRIAN STEAM ENGINE & CARRIAGE – LIVERPOOL & MANCHESTER RAILWAY

First published 2013

© Paul Leslie Line, 2013

Text © Paul Leslie Line

Maps and Photographs © as per credits on page 148.

Published by Mapseeker Archive Publishing Ltd, Mapseeker Studio, 30 High Street, Aldridge, Walsall, WS9 8LZ, Tel: +44 (0) 1922 288111 / +44 (0)1922 458288

Printed by Wyndeham Grange Ltd, Butts Road, Southwick, West Sussex, BN42 4EJ, 01273 592244

British Library Cataloguing in Publication Data.
A catalogue record for this book is available from the British Library.

ISBN 978-1-84491-798-3 Softcover
ISBN 978-1-84491-799-0 Hardcover

Typesetting and origination by Emily Benton & Adrian Baggett

Historical maps available to buy at
www.mapseeker.co.uk

CENTAUR STEAM ENGINE FROM THE GRAND JUNCTION RAILWAY 1838

ARMCHAIR TIME TRAVELLERS
RAILWAY ATLAS

FROM CANALS TO EARLY STEAM RAILWAYS
A HISTORY IN MAPS

MAPSEEKER ARCHIVE PUBLISHING

FOREWORD BY STUART WILLIAMS

ILLUSTRATED BY EMILY BENTON & ADRIAN BAGGETT

PUBLISHED & PRINTED IN ENGLAND

MAPSEEKER
ARCHIVE·PUBLISHING
GATEWAY TO OUR HISTORIC PAST
www.mapseeker.co.uk

FOREWORD

In the United Kingdom, we are fortunate to have on our very doorsteps at every turn the evidence of our own history, and the past greatness of this, the nation which was at the forefront of bringing about the modern age through the pursuit of science, engineering, industry and education.

It was the Industrial Revolution of c1760–1840 that kick-started this progress, and much of the world-wide success of the UK and the British Empire, now Commonwealth.

The most concrete evidence of that revolution is the remarkable transport network which was built firstly to support industry by enabling the easy transport of heavy goods and raw materials at a time when most roads were either poor or non-existent, and secondly to provide affordable and speedy public transport to allow people from all walks of life to travel the UK from top to bottom.

By the 1790s the canal network was at the heart of the Industrial Revolution, and quite literally formed the arteries of the nation. The phenomenal success of that venture is testament to the foresight and ingenuity of the canal builders, the great engineers and entrepreneurs of those days, and this was followed up by an even greater revolution when on the 15th of September 1830 George Stephenson finally opened the Liverpool to Manchester railway line.

While the coming of the steam railways inevitably signalled the long-term demise of the canal industry, it was to be even more significant for the progress of the United Kingdom, and despite the mistakes of the 1960s, the legacy of Stephenson and both his predecessors and successors remains with us today, at the heart of our lives, notably at a time when the modern road network, once seen as the doom of the railways, is becoming increasingly unworkable due to congestion.

This book offers a quite extraordinary insight into the history of that exciting and epoch-making period when this nation was the workshop of the world, using a remarkable panoply of period maps and illustrations, some attractively re-interpreted, and much fascinating and useful background information.

I heartily commend this work to the transport enthusiast, the cartographer, the historian and the lover of beautiful artwork alike.

Stuart Williams 2013

TAKING IN WATER AT PARKSIDE ON THE LIVERPOOL & MANCHESTER RAILWAY

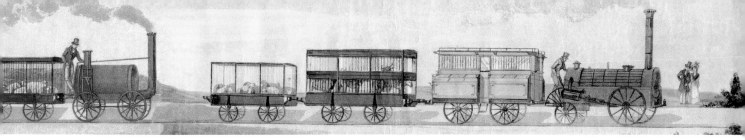

ACKNOWLEDGEMENTS

I would like to express my grateful thanks to everyone who has contributed to making this publication possible and those who have spent many hours passionately applying their skills and expertise, reflected in the completed work.

The Hon Sir William McAlpine Bt for kindly sourcing the base map templates in section four, originally prepared by I. James, former Inspector of Transport Police.

A special thanks to Matt Langham for his authorial contribution, especially in his work regarding George Stephenson and the development of the railway.

Stuart Williams – writer, historian and steam railway enthusiast – for his splendid foreword. Special thanks to Emily Benton for her illustrative work and many hours of design compilation, and Adrian Baggett for his illustrative skills and for finalising the design layout. Steve Toulouse and Phil Bradney for their many hours of meticulous and painstaking work digitally transforming the many antique original prints and antique town plans for the publication, Carla Johnston for her typesetting work, John and Julie Swann for supporting the editorial work and research.

Jonathan Gestetner for kindly sourcing two original antique plates used in the publication – Alken's illustrations of Modern Prophecy and the view along the Liverpool and Manchester Railway, top of pages six, seven, eight and nine.

Berian Williams and Steve Bartrick for sourcing additional antique views and vistas used in the book and Lynn Hughes for her wonderful pencil and charcoal drawing "The Stagecoaches".

Paul Leslie Line 2013

ENTRANCE OF THE RAILWAY AT EDGE HILL, LIVERPOOL – LIVERPOOL & MANCHESTER RAILWAY

INTRODUCTION

To most people today, the canal network is synonymous with leisurely pursuits – fishing, walking, narrowboat holidays; relaxing and mostly rural activities. The canal system is now a means to escape our modern, non-stop, urban lives. They are a refuge from the endless hustle and bustle of everyday life. Yet such pastoral appearances belie their true importance and rightful place in history. In the 1790s, the canal system was at the absolute core of British industry and was to remain so for a half-century. During this golden age, canals helped to fire the massive demands of the Industrial Revolution, the cornerstone and catalyst of our modern era.

This began with the pioneering Bridgewater Canal which was opened in 1761. Largely funded by Francis Egerton, the 3rd Duke of Bridgewater, it was designed by James Brindley and greatly eased the laborious task of hauling coal from Worsley's mines in north-west England to Manchester. Coal was the Industrial Revolution's most valuable commodity and base requirement – its "black gold" – and suddenly 10 times the amount of the mineral could be moved via horse drawn canal barges, more efficiently and at a faster speed to boot. The canal was considered the first true man-made waterway due to the inclusion of an aqueduct across the River Irwell, and its success was immediate and staggering both in financial and practical terms. The tolls that the Duke was able to charge for its use quickly recouped its massive construction costs – £168,000 at the time, nearly £24 million today. Its introduction meant that the massive fuel demands of the steam engines powering the swelling city of Manchester's factories were increasingly met, and the Industrial Revolution continued apace.

In 1783, Manchester had a single cotton mill and a population of 24,000. Just a generation of feverish production and industrial expansion later, the town had 86 mills drawing from a labour pool of 150,000, growth that was underpinned by the canal system. The profitability and success of the new form of transport prompted a period of "canal mania" as other entrepreneurs rushed to the marketplace. The network quickly expanded to become the world's first national one by the early 1820s and became a heavily used, vital hub of industry. Josiah Wedgewood, of Staffordshire pottery fame, used it to bring in hefty cargoes of clay to his factory doors, transporting the fragile finished product safely to market the other way.

It was an era far removed from the pedestrian connotations that canals have today. Before long, whole families lived near the waterways, dependent on the system for work. Navvies, the manual labourers who did the back-breaking, often dangerous graft of moving the earth during construction (later working on the railways) often found regular employment once they were completed. The network also employed toll-men, bridge and lock keepers whose jobs were to maintain and enforce the network's rules, save water and prevent damage to the locks. Canals' towpaths were well worn by horses' hooves towing barges, stopping at regular watering stations. By the 1790s, the pressure to move goods and people even lead to the introduction of "fly boats", express barges which travelled through the night on strict schedules and were given priority at locks and bridges.

By the turn of the 19th Century, the canal system seemed indispensable as it became increasingly woven into the fabric of society. Yet just as quickly as its importance had become seemingly unassailable, the canal was usurped by the invention that it had provided fuel for: the steam engine. Britain was to innovate in transport again, leading to massive social and economic upheavals fostered by the seemingly indomitable power of the Industrial Revolution.

While canals were a definite boon for industry, and marked real progress in moving freight, they were not without their drawbacks. A barge could move 25 tonnes of material, but even this struggled to keep up with the sheer volume of freight requiring transport by the early 1800s. Britain was pivotal in world trade at this point, in an economic climate where the pace of change was constantly increasing, with enormous pressure to remain at the top for prosperity and prestige. The canal owners held a steadfast monopoly on transport – only around 4% of boatmen even owned their own vessels – and ratcheted up profitability by raising tonnage fees. Their system was also subject to the climate – water could freeze in the winter and evaporate in the heat of high summer, the lowered canal levels easily grounding barges and disrupting trade. It was clear that a better solution was required, and was demanded by industrial leaders, to keep up with the rapid pace of change.

Inspiration was to come from an existing solution: the wagonways. These tracked routes were an important fixture, albeit on a smaller scale, and had been used to move coal by cart since the early 1700s. They benefited from the operation of a hard wheel turning on a hard, level track, which generated much less friction than a wheel being pulled on a poor quality road. The increased efficiency meant a horse could comfortably pull a cart with a 2.5 tonne load along with a wagon driver. At the turn of the 19th Century there were already some wagonways being powered by static steam engines, giving a massively increased pulling power – that of roughly 40 horses. Yet laying the tracks for such a system was time consuming, sometimes dangerous and inevitably expensive, such systems requiring a great deal of use before they could turn a profit.

Tracked routes were, however, seen as an increasingly good fit for the north west of England, an area that continued to experience a massive trade boom, with huge amounts of commodities – especially cotton – being regularly moved. The material arrived from overseas, from the Americas and the West

CONTENTS

THE DOUBLE LOCK & EAST ENTRANCE TO THE ISLINGTON TUNNEL, REGENTS CANAL

One
MAP OF THE CANALS OF
ENGLAND AND WALES 1809
– SHOWING SOME OF THE ESTABLISHED WAGONWAYS

The following pages in this section present a map of the canals of England and Wales towards the end of the first decade of the nineteenth century. At this point in history the canals had reached their zenith and were criss-crossing the country, connecting the many mining and manufacturing centres that were fostered by the Industrial Revolution and its impact on ever-growing towns and ports.

The table below lists the canals featured, with the corresponding reference number relating to the detailed map grid page. Importantly, this map also shows one or two of the early horse drawn wagonways, such as those at Ashby-de-la-Zouch. By the time this map was produced there were many of such routes in existence, where chaldron wagons full of coal or other materials were dragged along rails, originally made of wood, by horses between coal mines and loading-quays. These would become the stepping stone to the next revolution in travel and transportation – the steam driven railway.

Lancaster Canal	21	Wyrley and Essington Canal	26
Leeds and Liverpool Canal	21	Canal and Extension	26
Bradford Canal	21	Birmingham and Fazeley Canal	26
Huddersfield Canal	21	Worecester and Birmingham Canal	26
Bury and Ashton Canal	21	Droitwich Canal	26
Bolton Canal	21	Birmingham and Warwick Canal	26
Rochdale Canal	21	Stratford Canal	26
Peak Forest Canal	21	Ashby de la Zouch Canal	26
Grand Trunk or Trent and Mersey Canal	21	Coventry Canal	26
Chester Canal	21	Leicester Canal	26
Mount Weig'n Canal	22	Warwick and Napton Canal	26
Kingfton Upon Hill	22	Oxford Canal	26
Barnsley Canal	22	Thames and Severn Canal	26
Dearn and Dove Canal	22	Berks and Wilts Canal	26
Stainforth and Kadby Canal	22	Hereford and Gloucester Canal	26
Caistor Canal	22	Grantham Canal	27
Chesterfield Canal	22	Oakham Canal	27
Montgomery Canal	25	Wisbeach Canal	27
Ellesmere Canal	25	Grand Junction Canal	27
Shrewsbury Canal	25	Paddington Canal	27
Kington Canal	25	Great Western Canal	31
Hereford and Glocester Canal	25	Kennet and Avon Canal	32
Brecknock Canal	25	Somerset Canal	32
Swansea Canal	25	Salisbury Canal	32
Neath Canal	25	Andover Canal	32
Aberdare Canal	25	Dorset and Somerset Canal	32
Cardiff Canal	25	Basingstoke Canal	33
Monmouthshire Canal	25	Great Surrey Canal	33
Donnington Wood Canal	26	Rochester Canal	33
Stafford and Worcester Canal	26		

CANALS AND WAGONWAYS OF ENGLAND AND WALES 1809

KEY TO MAP PAGES

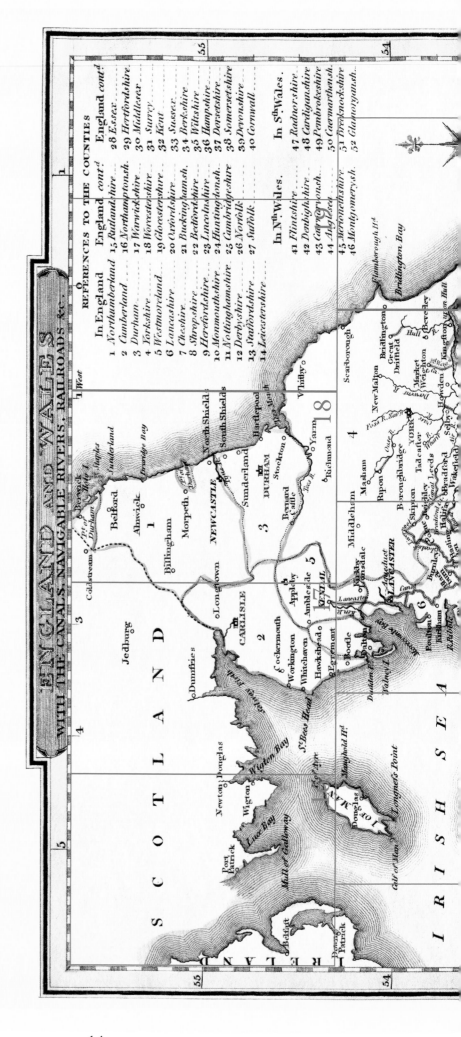

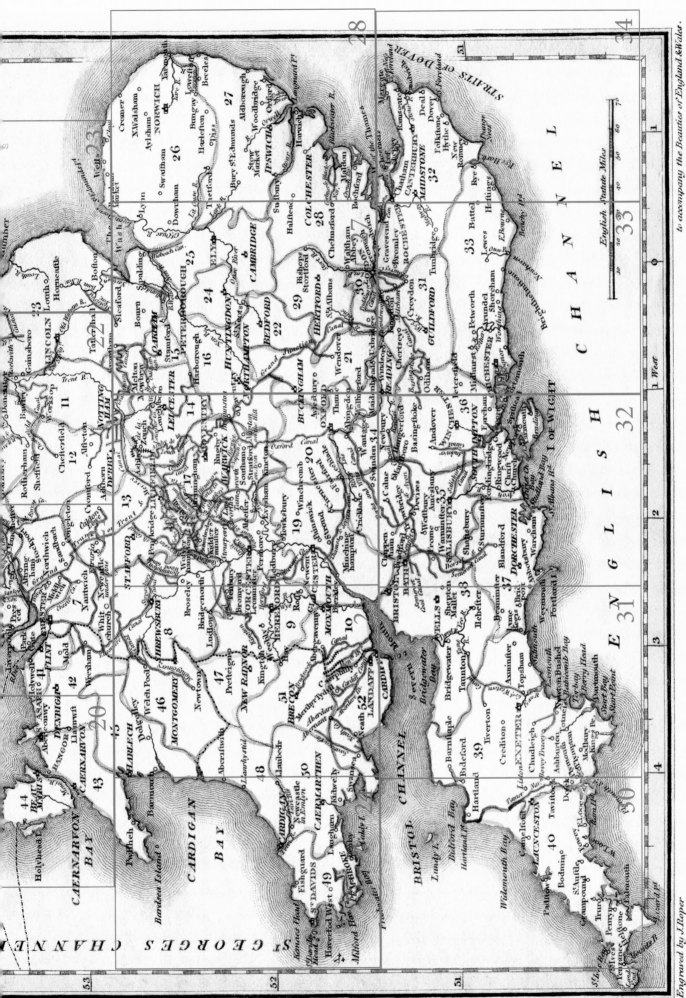

London, Published for the Proprietors, by Vernor, Hood and Sharpe, Poultry, Dec.r 1.st 1809.

to accompany the Beauties of England & Wales.

Engraved by J. Roper.

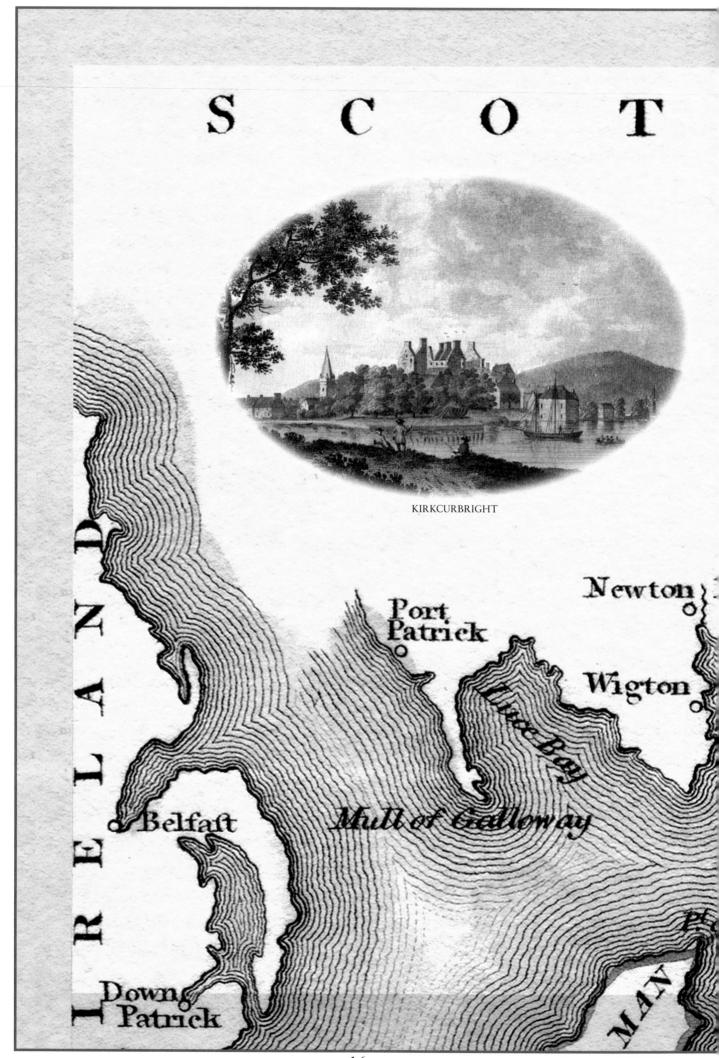

S   C   O   T

KIRKCURBRIGHT

Newton

Wigton

Port
Patrick

Luce Bay

I
R
E
L
A
N
D

Belfast

Mull of Galloway

Down
Patrick

MAN

16

Go to page 20 ▽

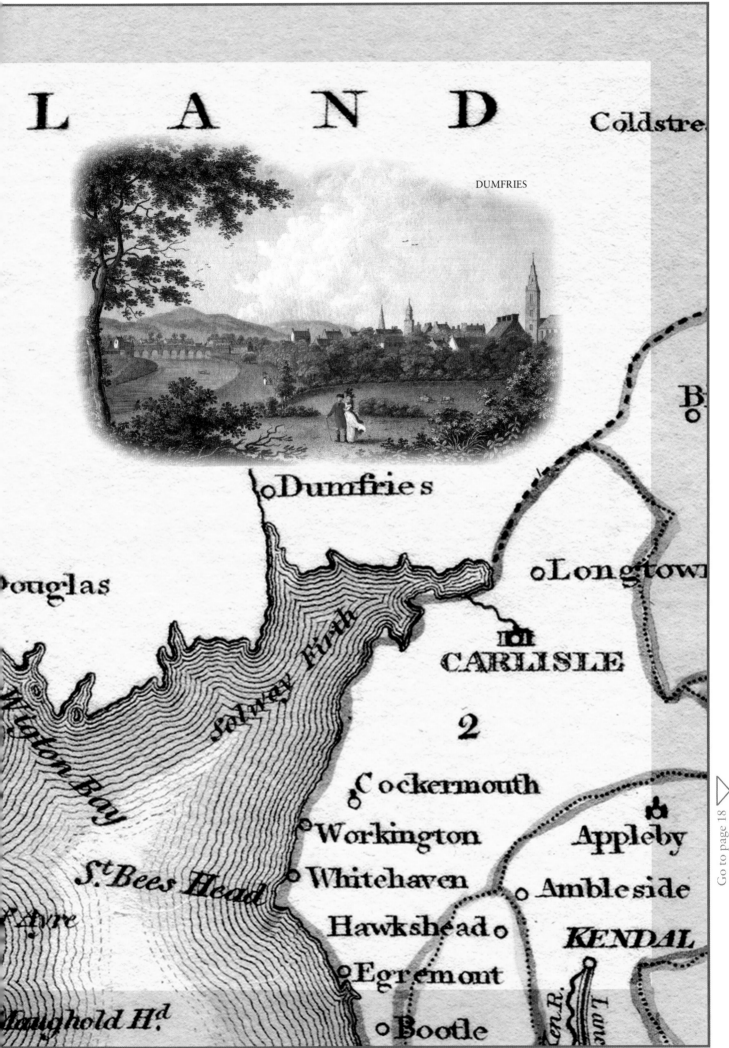

L A N D

DUMFRIES

B

o Dumfries

Douglas

o Longtow

Salway Firth

CARLISLE

2

Wigton Bay

Cockermouth

o Workington   Appleby

St Bees Head   o Whitehaven   Ambleside

Hawkshead o   KENDAL

Ayre

o Egremont

Maughold Hd.

o Bootle

Cen.R.

Lane.

Go to page 18 ▷

Go to page 21 ▽

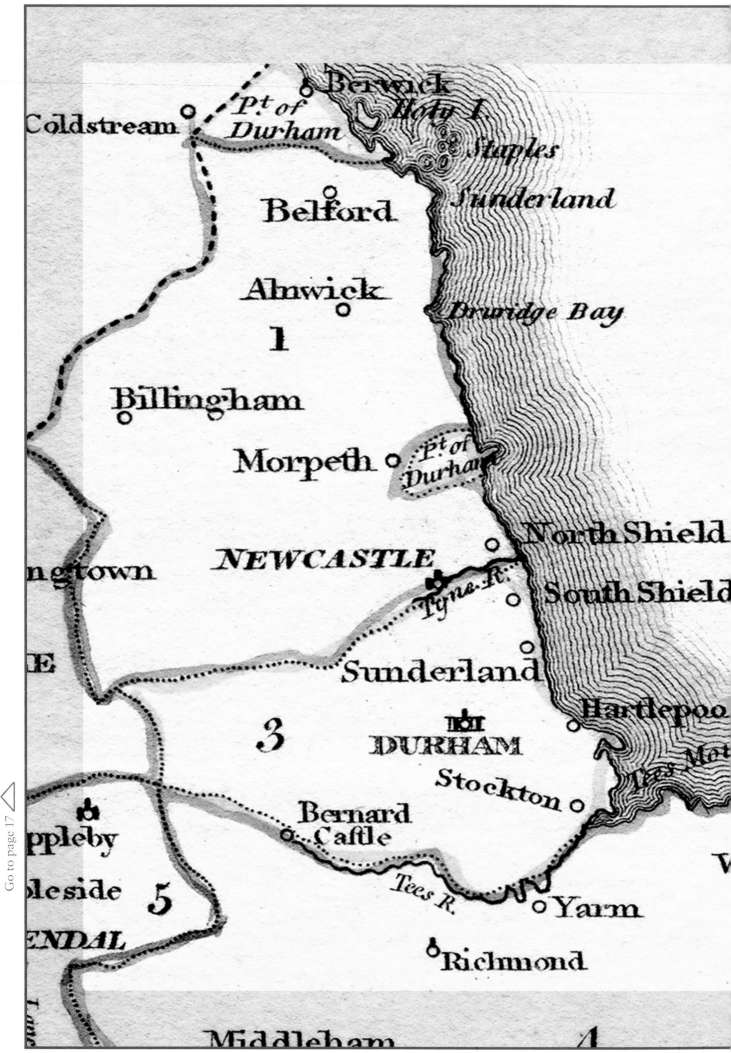

Go to page 17

Go to page 22

Go to page 17

KENDAL

Egremont

Bootle

Dalton

Ken R.

dden I.

Walney I.

Lancaster

Kirkby Lonsdale

Middleham

Ripon

---Aqueduct
LANCASTER

Borou

Morecambe Bay

Canal

6

Leeds & Liverpool

Skipton

Colne

Keighley

Poulton

Kirkham

Burnley

Bradford Ca.

R. Ribble

Black burn

Hasling-den

Halifax

B

Leeds & Liverpool

Ormskirk

Wigan

or Bury Ex.

Hasting.

Rochdale Canal

Hudd-field

A

Houghton

Bolton

Bury G.

Ashton C.

Huddersfield Can.

Marsey R.

Leigh

Manchester

B

Liverpool

sanker

Prescot

Altring-ham

Stockport

Peak Forest Ca.

Ro

Park

Gate

Weaver Ro

Grand

Northwich

Holywell

41

FLINT

CHESTER

Middle wich

Sandbach

Congleton

Chester Ca.

Mold

Caldon Lowe

Crom

42

7

Nantwich

Etruria

Trunk or Tre

Wrexham

Ellesmere

Whit church

Newcastle *under Line*

STAFFORD

13

Ash

Go to page 22

Go to page 25

Go to page 18

Go to page 21

Go to page 26

Go to page 22 △

Go to page 28 ▷

Go to page 33 ▽

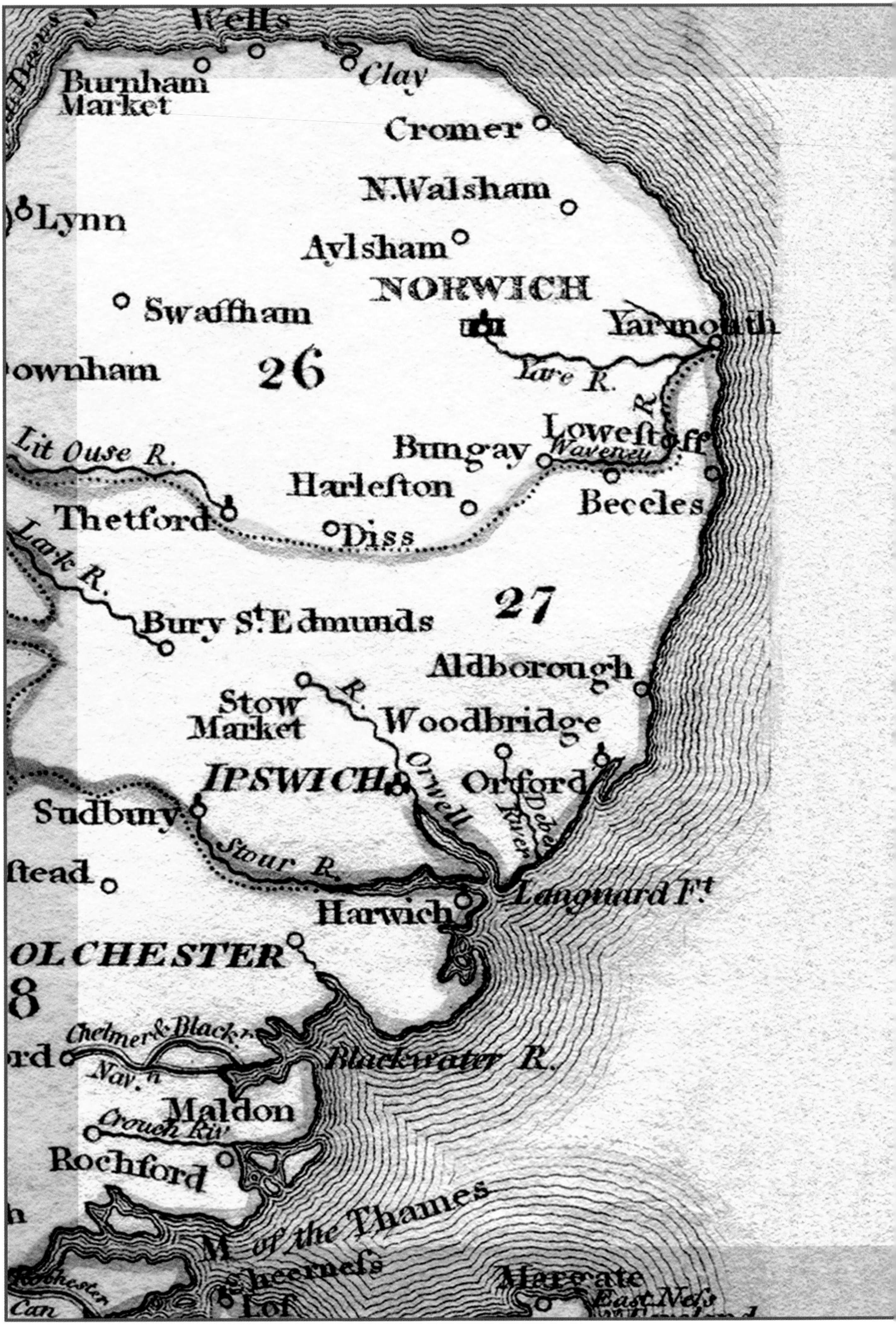

Wells

Burnham
Market

Clay

Cromer

N.Walsham

Lynn

Aylsham

NORWICH

Swaffham

Yarmouth

ownham

26

Yare R.

Lit Ouse R.

Bungay

Waveney

Loweftoff

R.

Harleston

Lark R.

Thetford

Diss

Beccles

Bury St. Edmunds

27

Aldborough

Stow
Market

R.

Woodbridge

IPSWICH

Orwell

Orford

Sudbury

Deben River

ftead

Stour R.

Langnard Ft

Harwich

OLCHESTER

8

Go to page 27 ◁

Chelmer & Black.n

Blackwater R.

rd

Nav.n

Maldon

Crouch Riv.

Rochford

M. of the Thames

Rocheſter

heerneſs

Margate

Can

I. of

East Neſs

28

Go to page 27

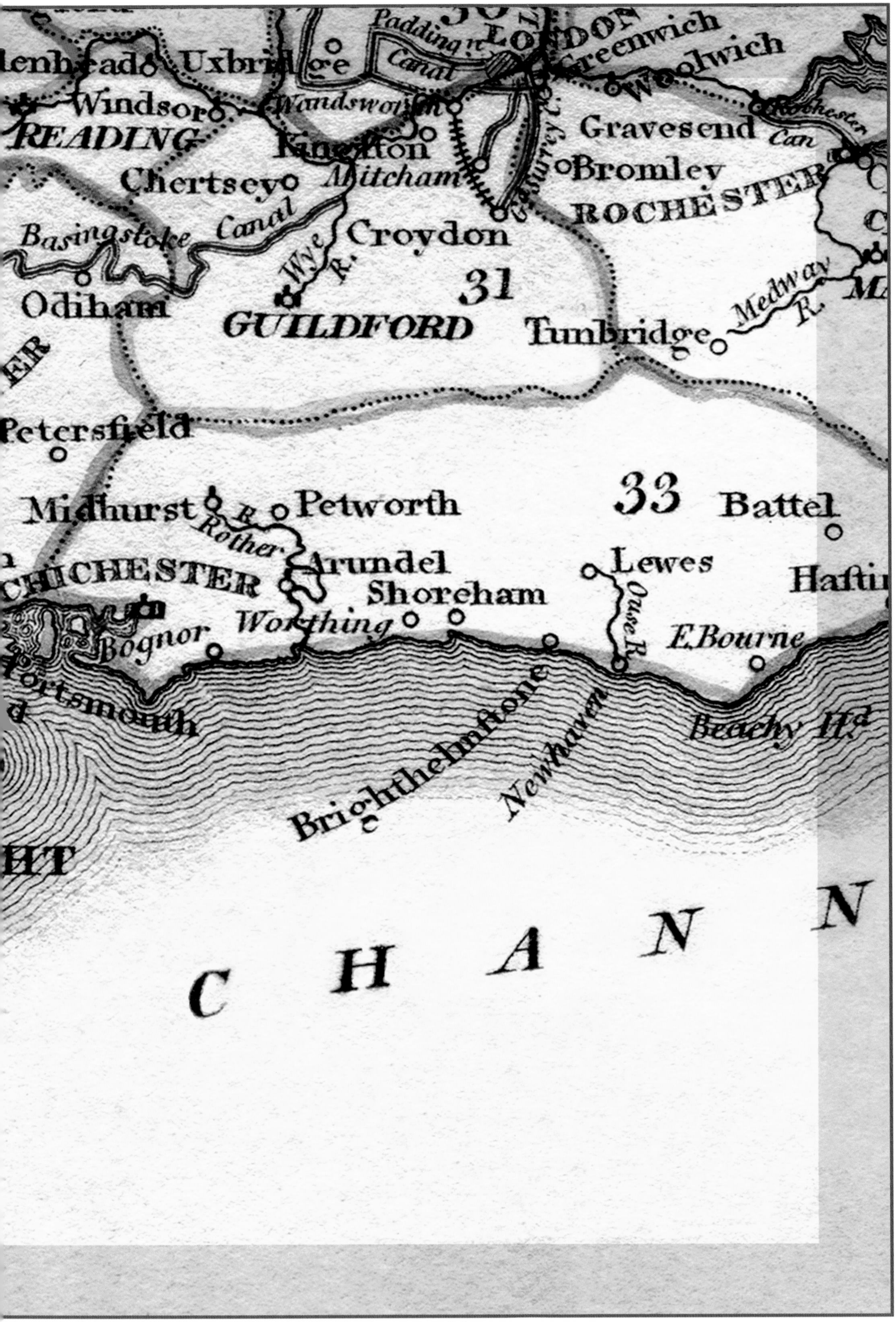

lenhead○ Uxbridge

Windsor

READING

Kingston

Chertsey○ Mitcham

Wandsworth

Paddington Canal

LONDON

Greenwich Woolwich

Gravesend

Bromley

ROCHESTER

Grand Surrey Canal

Rochester Can

Basingstoke Canal

Odiham

Wye R.

Croydon

31

GUILDFORD

Tunbridge

Medway R.

Ma

Petersfield○

Midhurst

Rother R.

Petworth

33

Battel○

CHICHESTER

Arundel

Shoreham

Worthing

Lewes

Ouse R.

E. Bourne

Hasti

Bognor

Portsmouth

Brighthelmstone

Newhaven

Beachy Hd.

HT

C H A N N

3 3

Go to page 34

Go to page 28 △

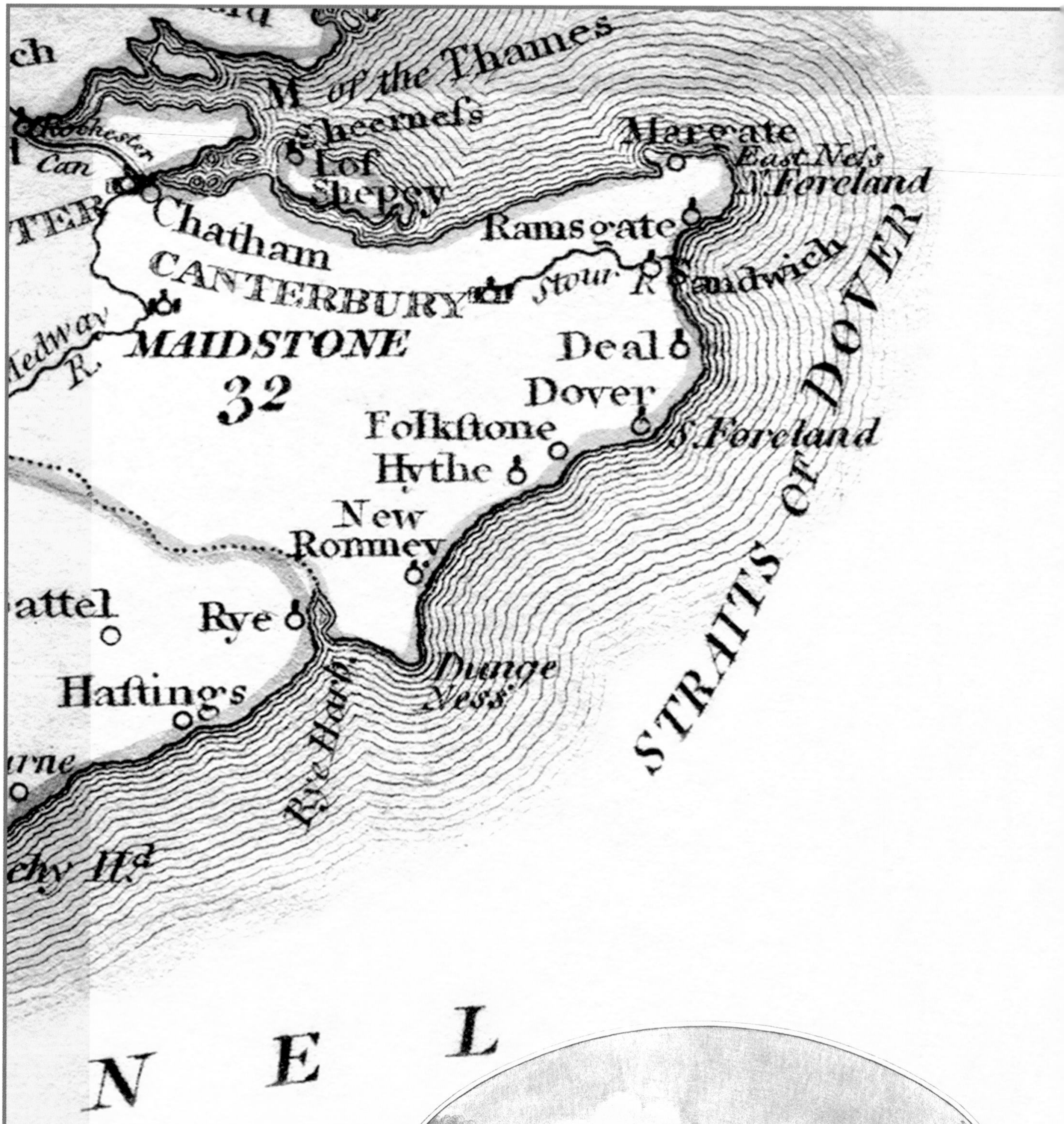

ch

M of the Thames

Rochester
Can

Sheernefs

I of
Shepey

Mergate

East Nefs
N Foreland

Chatham

CANTERBURY

Ramsgate

Stour R Sandwich

MAIDSTONE

Deal

Medway R

32

Dover

S Foreland

Folkstone

Hythe

New
Romney

attel

Rye

Rye Harb

Dunge
Ness

STRAITS or DOVER

Hastings

urne

chy IId

N E L

Go to page 33 ◁

ENTRANCE TO HASTINGS BY THE LONDON ROAD

WO
EARLY ENGLISH TOWN PLANS BEFORE THE ARRIVAL OF THE RAILWAYS

The town plans in this section offer a final glimpse of many of Britain's towns and cities before their landscapes were significantly and irrevocably altered by the arrival of the railway. For some places the upheaval was dramatic, with entire streets being levelled – as seen in Birmingham – and many of these views are of surprisingly rural vistas that are now lost. Large, man-made feats of civil engineering and construction came to dominate urban views in the form of viaducts, aqueducts and high level railway bridges, as seen in the bridge over the Tyne at Newcastle. Suburbanisation coupled with industrial and population growth on an unprecedented scale saw the larger manufacturing towns expand rapidly, consuming outlying villages within a few decades and forming large industrial conurbations by the end of the nineteenth century.

The majority of these plans were originally created by John Roper and George Cole. Roper was an English engraver, known to have worked from several locations in London, and he crafted the maps, drawn by Cole, to accompany Edward W. Brayley and John Britton's part-work entitled "Beauties of England and Wales". This was published in 18 volumes between c.1804 and 1810 and as "The British Atlas" in 1810 by Verner, Hood and Sharpe. Roper's maps were also reissued to illustrate the Reverend J. Nightingale's "English Topography" of 1816 (and other later editions), published by Baldwin, Craddock and Joy – another publishing partnership of the nineteenth century.

HIGH LEVEL BRIDGE AT NEWCASTLE OPENED IN 1849

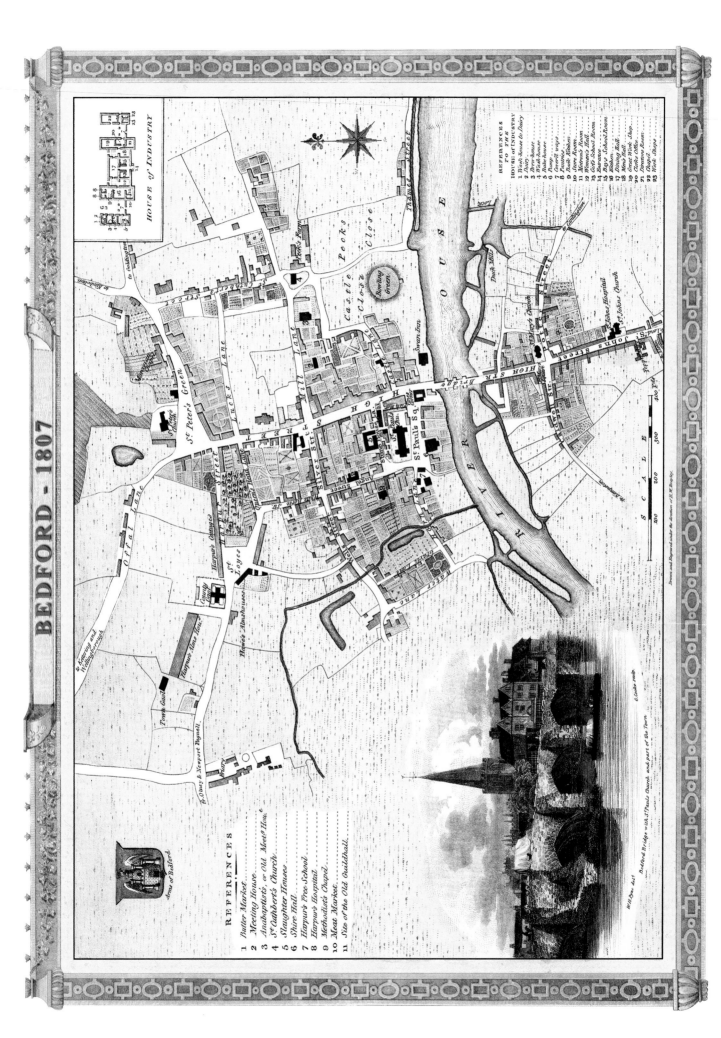

BEDFORD - 1807

Arms of Bedford

REFERENCES

1 Butter Market
2 Meeting House
3 Anabaptists, or Old Meet.g Hou.e
4 St Cuthbert's Church
5 Slaughter Houses
6 Shire Hall
7 Harpur's Free School
8 Harpur's Hospital
9 Methodist's Chapel
10 Meat Market
11 Site of the Old Guildhall

REFERENCES TO THE HOUSE of INDUSTRY

1 Wash-house to Dairy
2 Dairy
3 Brew-house
4 Wash-house
5 Bake-house
6 Pump
7 Gravell ways
8 Pantries
9 Maids Kitchen
10 Store Room
11 Metron's Room
12 Woman's Hall
13 Girls School Room
14 Entrance
15 Boy's School Room
16 Kitchen
17 Dining Hall
18 Men's Hall
19 Great Work Shop
20 Clerk's Office
21 Directors Room
22 Chapel
23 Work Shops

HOUSE of INDUSTRY

Drawn and Engraved under the direction of B.W. Brayley.

Bedford Bridge with St Pauls Church and part of the Town.

38

PLAN OF BIRMINGHAM - 1805

Drawn by
J.ˢ SHERRIFF
of Oldswinford
late of the Crescent
BIRMINGHAM.

REFERENCE
A St Martin's Church.
B St Philip's Church.
C St Barthol.ˢ Chapel.
D St Mary's Chapel.
E St Paul's Chapel.
F St John's Chapel.
G New - Meeting.
H Old - Meeting.
I Free School.
J Theatre.
K Charity School.
L Moat House.
M Quakers Meeting.

REFERENCE
1 The Square
2 Colmore Row
3 Temple Row
4 Edmund St.
5 St Paul's Square
6 Caroline St.
7 Church Street
8 Congreve St.
9 Paradise St.
10 Hill Street
11 Horse Fair
12 Smalbrook St.
13 Bull Ring
14 Moseley Street
15 Aulcester St.
16 Bordesley Street
17 Bartholomew St.
18 Great Brooke St.
19 Temple St.

CAMBRIDGE - 1804

Kings College Chapel. *University Library* *the Senate House*

REFERENCE.

1 *Magdalen Coll. & Lodge*
2 *St. John's Coll.*
3 *Trinity Coll.*
4 *Gonville & Caius Coll.*
5 *Trinity Hall*
6 *Clare Hall*
7 *King's Coll. & Chapel*
8 *Catherine Hall*
9 *Queen's Coll.*
10 *Peter House Coll. & Lodge*
11 *Pembroke Hall*
12 *Corpus Christi Coll.*
13 *Jesus Coll.*
14 *Sidney Sussex Coll.*
15 *Christ Coll.*
16 *Emanuel Coll.*
17 *Senate House*
18 *Public Schools & Library*
19 *St. Giles' Church*
20 *St. Clement's Church*
21 *St. Sepulchre's Church*
22 *All Saints Church*
23 *St. Michael's Church*
24 *Gr.t St. Mary's Church*
25 *Lit. St. Mary's Church*
26 *Trinity Church*
27 *St. Andrew's Church*
28 *St. Peter's Church*
29 *St. Benet's Church*
30 *St. Botolph's Church*
31 *St. Edward's Church*
32 *Town Hall*
33 *The Free School*
34 *Anabaptist's Meet.g Hou.*
35 *Shire Hall*

Arms of the University *Arms of Cambridge*

SCALE

Drawn and Engraved under the direction of J. Britton, & E.W. Brayley.

CANTERBURY - 1806

SCALE ¼ of a Mile.

Drawn and Engraved under the direction of E.W.Brayley.

41

CARLISLE - 1805

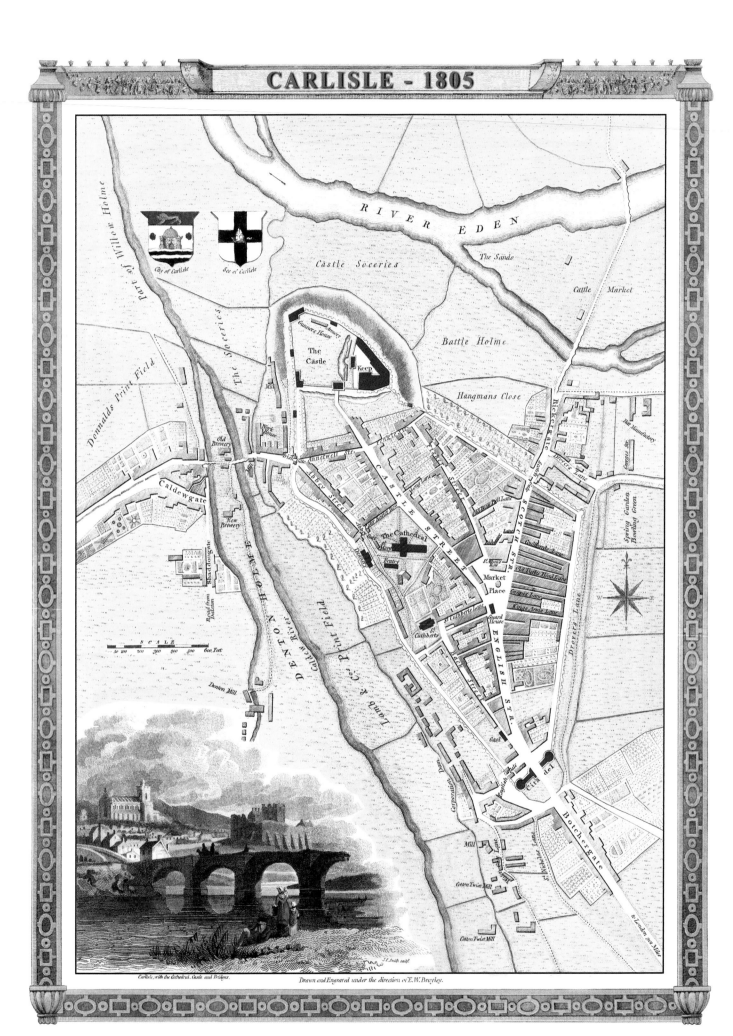

RIVER EDEN

City of Carlisle · See of Carlisle

Part of Willow Holme

Dennalds Print Field

The Soceries

Castle Soceries

The Sands

Castle Market

Battle Holme

Gunners House · Armory

The Castle · Keep

Hangmans Close

Rickergate

Pat Manufactory

Caxgate Str.

Brewery Lane

Work House

Old Brewery

Caldewgate

Irish gate · Annetwell Str.

Finkle Str.

Scotch Str.

Spring Garden Bowling Green

New Brewery

Shaddongate

Abbey Street

King Lane

CASTLE STREET

Market Bell Lane

Old Parke Head Lane

Road from Dalston

Caldew or Denton HOLME

Denton River

Abbey Gate

The Cathedral

St. Marys Row

Prestry

The Cathedral

St. Albans Row

Market Place

Cogness Lane

Kings Arms Lane

Drovers Lane

Denton Mill

Lamb & Cos Print Field

Corporation Dam

St. Cuthberts

St Cuthberts Lane

Back Street

ENGLISH STR.

Guard House

Gaol

Citadel

English Gate

Mill

Abraham St.

Botchergate

Mill Lane

Cotton Twist Mill

Cotton Twist Mill

To London 300 Miles

SCALE
50 100 200 300 400 500 600 Feet

Carlisle, with the Cathedral, Castle and Bridges.

Drawn and Engraved under the direction of E.W.Brayley.

J.C.Smith sculpt.

42

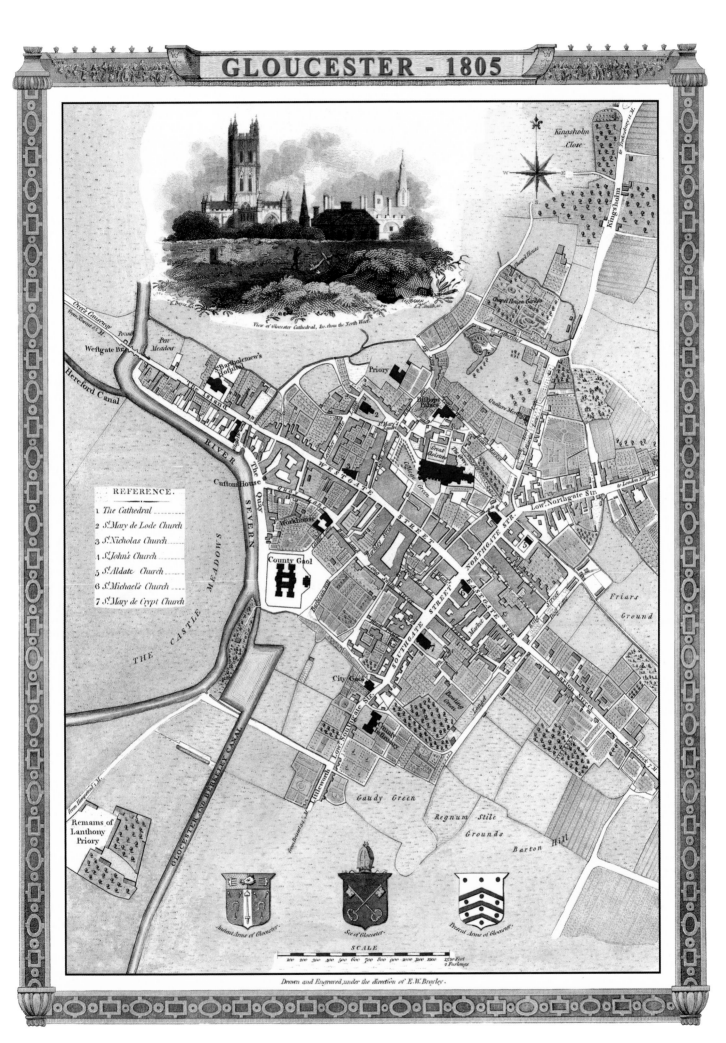

GLOUCESTER - 1805

View of Gloucester Cathedral, &c. from the North West.

REFERENCE.
1 The Cathedral
2 St. Mary de Lode Church
3 St. Nicholas Church
4 St. John's Church
5 St. Aldate Church
6 St. Michael's Church
7 St. Mary de Crypt Church

Ancient Arms of Gloucester.

See of Gloucester.

Present Arms of Gloucester.

SCALE
100 200 300 400 500 600 700 800 900 1000 1100 1200   1300 Feet
2 Furlongs

Drawn and Engraved, under the direction of E.W. Brayley.

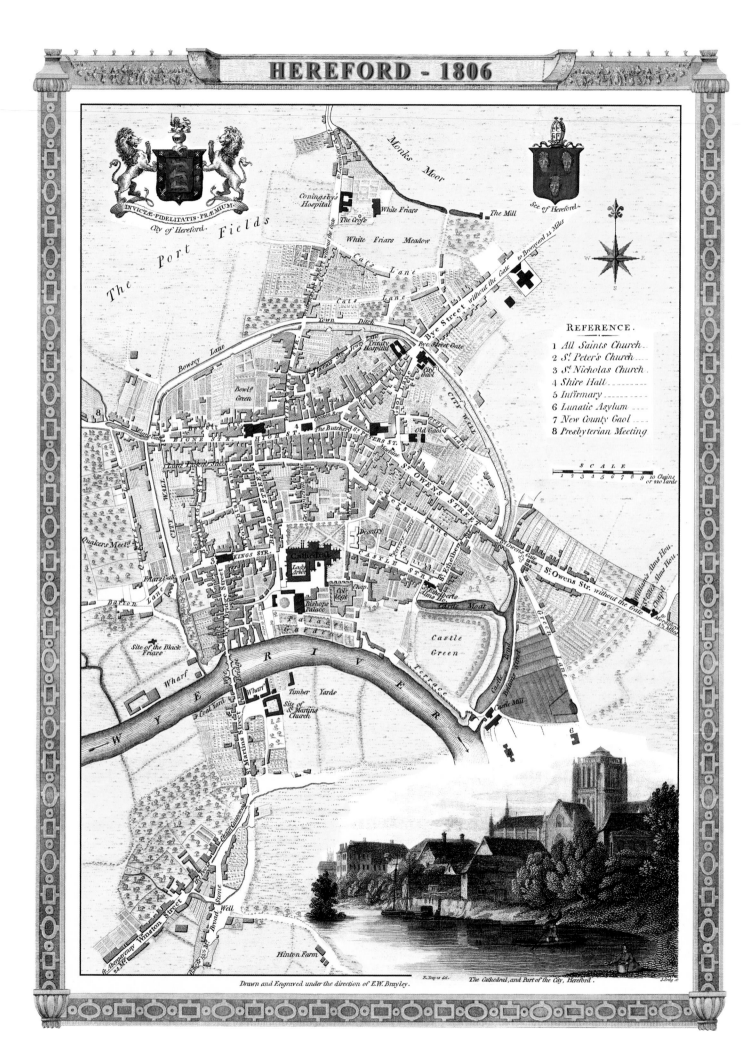

HEREFORD - 1806

INVICTÆ·FIDELITATIS·PRÆMIUM.

City of Hereford.

See of Hereford.

Monks Moor

The Port Fields

Coningsby's Hospital

The Cross

White Friars

The Mill

White Friars Meadow

Cats Lane

Cats Lane

to Bromyard 14 Miles

Bye Street without the Gate

Town Ditch

Bowsey Lane

Thomas Str

Jewy Lane

Trinity Hospital

Bye Street Gate

City Wall

Bye Str

City Goal

CITY WALL

Bowl? Green

Oyster Row

EIGN STR

4 ST

The Butcher St

St PETERS ST.

Machine Lane

Old Goal

Old Gaol

Eign Gate

8

ST. OWENS STREET

Blue School Str.

SCALE

1 2 3 4 5 6 7 8 9 10 Chains
or 220 Yards

Little Packers Street

Quakers Meet?

Friars Gate

3

KINGS STR.

Cathedral

Lady Arbor

Deanery

Packers Lane

CASTLE STR.

St Ethelberts

Castle Lane

St Owens Gate

St. Owens Str. without the Gate

William's Alms Hou.

St Giles's Alms Hou.

Chapel

Barton Lane

Col-lege

Chap.

St Ethelberts Alms Ho.

Castle Moat

Green Lane

Site of the Black Friars

Bishops Palace

Palace Gardens

Castle Green

Castle Pond

Britains creek

St Owens Gate

Wye Bridge Street

WYE RIVER

Wharf

Terrace

Castle Mill

6

Wharf

Coal Yard

Timber Yards

St Martins Street

Site of St Martins Church

RIVER

Chain Causeway

Broad Well

To Ross 13 M?

To Abergavenny 24 M?

Winston Street

Broad Stone

Hinton Farm

Drawn and Engraved under the direction of E.W. Brayley.

E. Dayes del.

The Cathedral, and Part of the City, Hereford.

REFERENCE.

1 All Saints Church
2 St. Peter's Church
3 St. Nicholas Church
4 Shire Hall
5 Infirmary
6 Lunatic Asylum
7 New County Gaol
8 Presbyterian Meeting

LANCASTER – 1824

REFERENCES.
St Mary's Church..... 1
St John's Chapel..... 2
Friends Meet House... 3
Independent Chapel... 4
Presbyterian. D°..... 5
Catholic. D°..... 6
Methodist. D°..... 7
Town Hall..... 8
Bank..... 9
Dispensary..... 10
News Room..... 11
Assembly D°..... 12
PennyHospital..... 13
Gillbeens D°..... 14
Post Office..... 15
Barton House..... 16
BoysNationalSch¹..... 17
Girls. D°..... 18

Surveyed, 1824.

Scale of Feet.
50 100 200 400 600

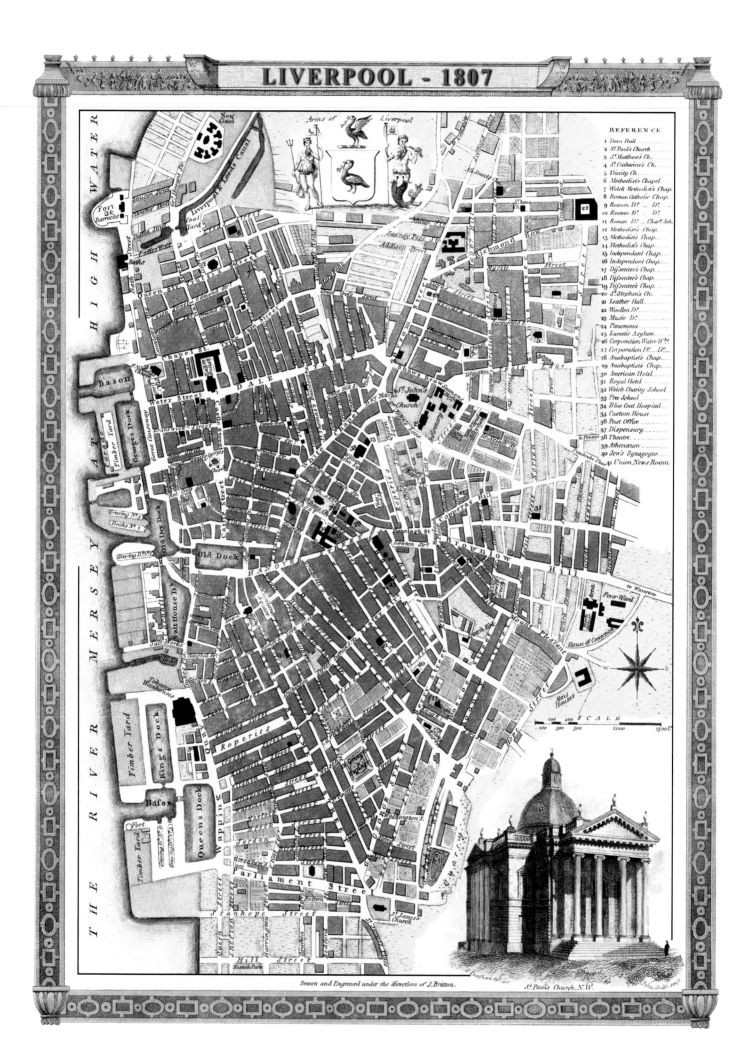

LIVERPOOL - 1807

Arms of Liverpool

REFERENCE

1 Town Hall
2 St Paul's Church
3 St Matthew's Ch.
4 St Catharine's Ch.
5 Trinity Ch.
6 Methodist's Chapel
7 Welch Methodist's Chap.
8 Roman Catholic Chap.
9 Roman Do. — Do.
10 Roman Do. — Do.
11 Roman Do. — Char.d Sch.
12 Methodist's Chap.
13 Methodist's Chap.
14 Methodist's Chap.
15 Independant Chap.
16 Independant Chap.
17 Difsenter's Chap.
18 Difsenter's Chap.
19 Difsenter's Chap.
20 St Stephen's Ch.
21 Leather Hall
22 Woollen Do.
23 Music Do.
24 Panorama
25 Lunatic Asylum
26 Corporation Water Wks
27 Corporation Do. Do.
28 Anabaptist's Chap.
29 Anabaptist's Chap.
30 American Hotel
31 Royal Hotel
32 Welch Charity School
33 Free School
34 Blue Coat Hospital
35 Custom House
36 Post Office
37 Dispensary
38 Theatre
39 Athenæum
40 Jew's Synagogue
41 Union News Room

SCALE

Drawn and Engraved under the direction of J. Bratton.

St Pauls Church. N.W.

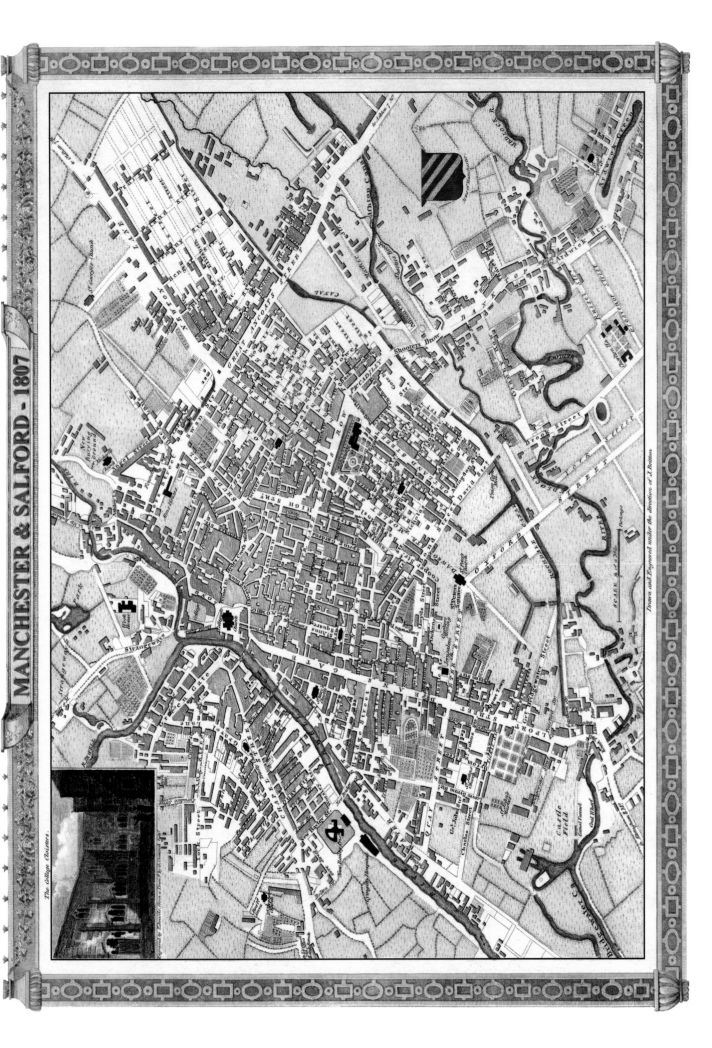

MANCHESTER & SALFORD – 1807

The College Cloisters.

Drawn and Engraved under the direction of J. Britton.

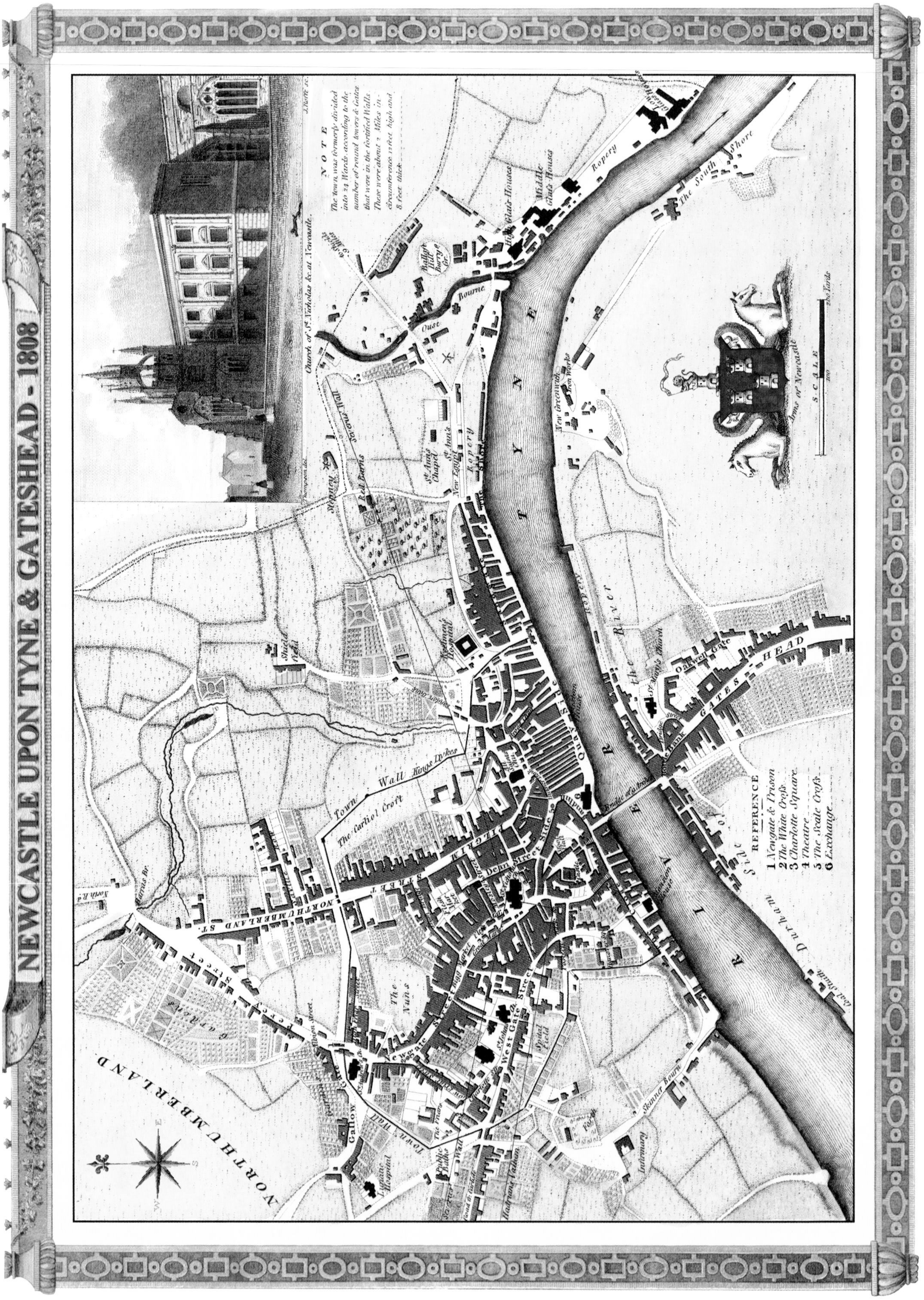

NEWCASTLE UPON TYNE & GATESHEAD - 1808

NOTE

The town was formerly divided into 24 Wards according to the number of round towers & Gates that were on the fortified Walls These were about 2 Miles in circumference in the high and 8 feet thick

Church of St Nicholas &c at Newcastle

REFERENCE

1 Newgate & Prison
2 The White Cross
3 Charlotte Square
4 Theatre
5 The State Cross
6 Exchange

SCALE

Ions or Newcastle

Yards

NORTHUMBERLAND

TYNE

The River

The South Shore

GATESHEAD

Durham

Town Wall

The Carliol Croft

Kings Dykes

NORTHUMBERLAND ST.

The Nuns

West Gate

Dean Street

Bourne

Ouse

Ropery

Middle Glass Houses

The Greenwich

Iron Works

Oakwell Gate

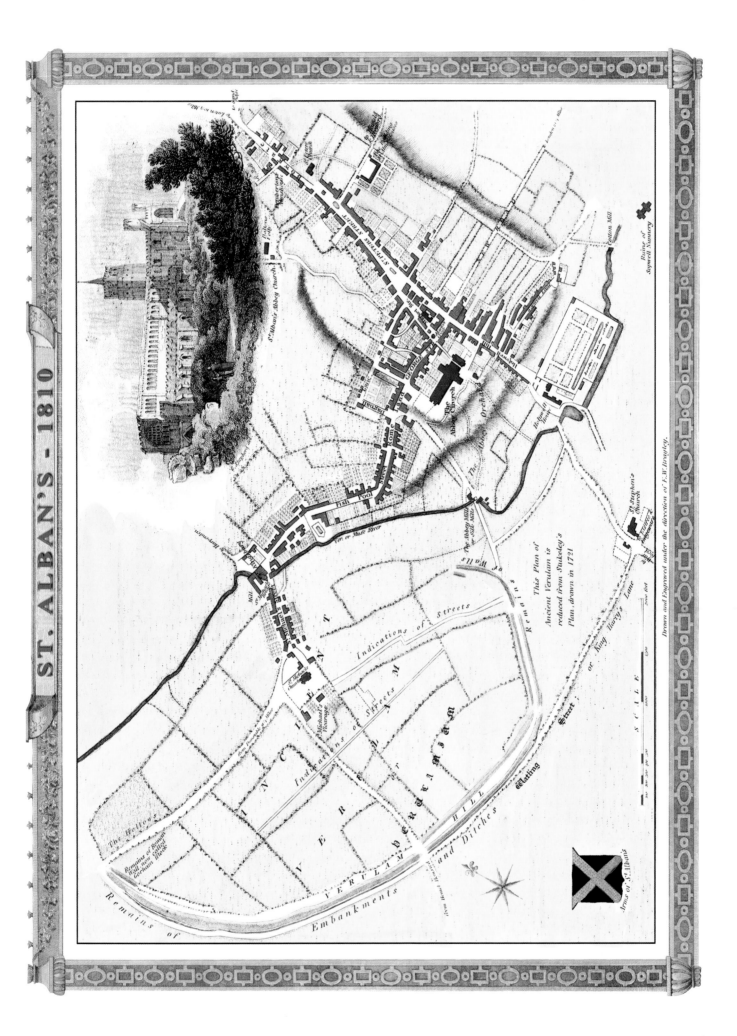

ST. ALBAN'S - 1810

St. Albans Abbey Church

St. Peters Street

The Abbey Orchard

Ruins of
Sopwell Nunnery

St. Stephens Church

This Plan of
Ancient Verulam is
reduced from Stukeley's
Plan, drawn in 1721

Indications of Streets

Indications of Streets

Remains of Roman
wall now called
Gorham Block

The Hollows

VERULAM HILL

Remains of Embankments and Ditches

Drawn and Engraved under the direction of F.W.Brayley.

SCALE

Arms of St. Albans

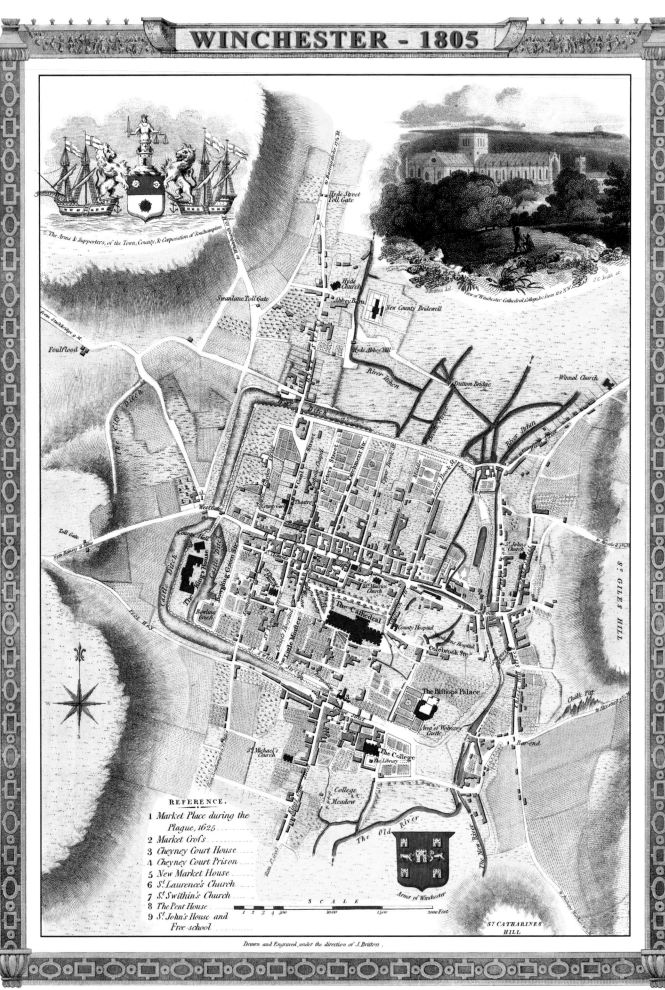

WINCHESTER - 1805

The Arms & Supporters, of the Town, County, & Corporation of Southampton

View of Winchester Cathedral College &c. from the N.W.

J. Britton del.   J.C. Smith sc.

REFERENCE.

1 *Market Place during the*
   Plague, 1625
2 *Market Cross*
3 *Cheyney Court House*
4 *Cheyney Court Prison*
5 *New Market House*
6 *St Laurence's Church*
7 *St Swithin's Church*
8 *The Pent House*
9 *St John's House and*
   Free school

SCALE

1 2 3 4 500   1000   1500   2000 Feet

Arms of Winchester

ST CATHARINES HILL

Drawn and Engraved, under the direction of J. Britton.

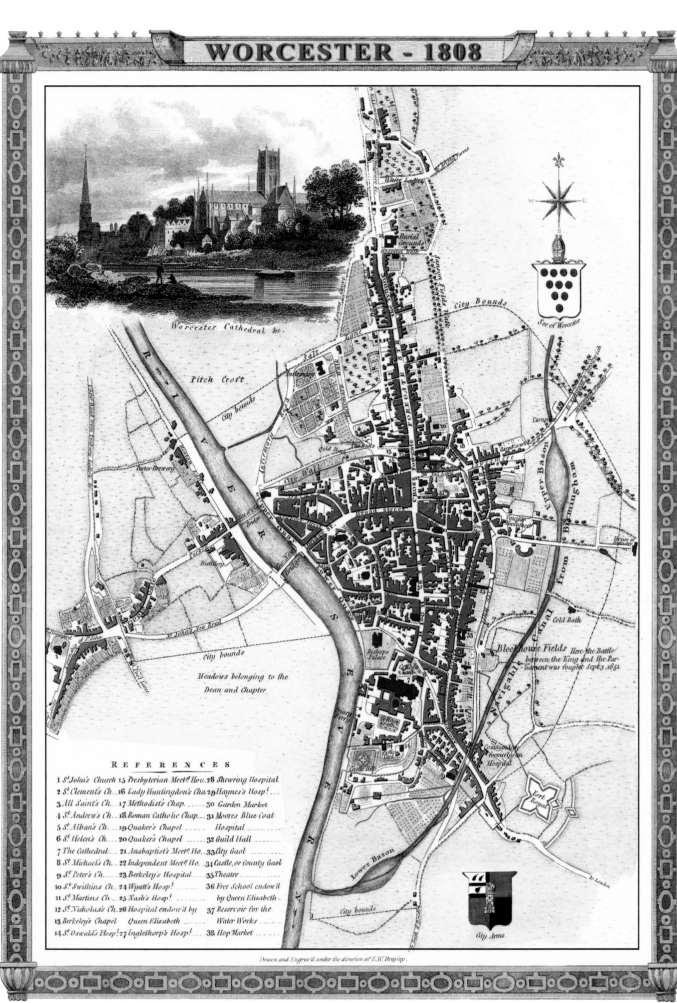

WORCESTER - 1808

Worcester Cathedral &c.

See of Worcester

City Arms

REFERENCES

1 St. John's Church	15 Presbyterian Meet.g Hou.	28 Shewring Hospital
2 St. Clement's Ch.	16 Lady Huntingdon's Cha.	29 Haynes's Hosp.l
3 All Saint's Ch.	17 Methodist's Chap.	30 Garden Market
4 St. Andrew's Ch.	18 Roman Catholic Chap.	31 Moores Blue Coat
5 St. Alban's Ch.	19 Quaker's Chapel	Hospital
6 St. Helen's Ch.	20 Quaker's Chapel	32 Guild Hall
7 The Cathedral	21 Anabaptist's Meet.g Ho.	33 City Gaol
8 St. Michael's Ch.	22 Independent Meet.g Ho.	34 Castle, or County Gaol
9 St. Peter's Ch.	23 Berkeley's Hospital	35 Theatre
10 St. Swithins Ch.	24 Wyatt's Hosp.l	36 Free School endow'd
11 St. Martins Ch.	25 Nash's Hosp.l	by Queen Elizabeth
12 St. Nicholas's Ch.	26 Hospital endow'd by	37 Reservoir for the
13 Berkeley's Chapel	Queen Elizabeth	Water Works
14 St. Oswald's Hosp.l	27 Inglethorp's Hosp.l	38 Hop Market

Drawn and Engrav'd under the direction of E.W. Brayley.

Three

GEORGE STEPHENSON AND THE DEVELOPMENT OF THE RAILWAY

The idea of connecting the two important industrial hubs of Liverpool and Manchester by means of a wagonway, with trains conveying goods by horse power, was first proposed by William Jessop in 1797. In 1800, he and Benjamin Outram made a survey of the land between Liverpool and Manchester, hoping to find a route that would be as short and level as possible. However, two factors prevented their progress: the Bridgewater Canal, which was well established and dominating the region, and the uncertainty surrounding the steam engine's potential. Could it really be developed into a reliable and efficient system, replacing the canal?

George Stephenson's role in the development and implementation of the railway is well documented, with his achievements in harnessing the power of steam kick-starting a revolution in transport and, ultimately, British life, ushering in the modern era. Yet what is given markedly less attention is the fact that he was uniquely positioned to do this, coming to prominence at just the right time, with the abilities, personality, ideas and, crucially, support – directly or indirectly from his peers' accomplishments – which gave him the opportunity to pave the way for a more progressive age of transport. Whilst this book is dedicated to Stephenson as a pioneer, and hopefully serves as a humble testament to his genius, this section explores the period in which he lived and worked more fully. Placing his feats in context casts fresh light on those names now often sidelined as footnotes in history, but who played important roles in the development of the railway, which has a long, interesting and frequently unconventional history.

The kernel of an idea that was to become the railway lay in the wagonways. These were wooden, but also occasionally iron, routes of tracks which have a common source: their rise and first application being found in the British mining industry. Dispersed around the country, colliery owners independently happened upon them as the best possible solution to an established problem, namely that of the transportation of coal from the pits to ports or industrial centres, with the loaded carts being drawn by horses with relative ease and efficiency. However, this system was often ramshackle; a merely serviceable means to an end that predated the Industrial Revolution by some time, being well established and conventional by the beginning of the period. Records dating their introduction accurately do not exist, although it is known that a Master Beaumont laid down wooden rails as early as 1630 to link his pits in Newcastle with the banks of the Tyne and water transport, but it is likely that the idea predates even this; it is said that German miners digging for copper in England's Lake District in the 1560s used wagons on rails for ease of access into the mines.

Local landowners approved of Beaumont's system – despite the inconvenience they were able to make use of their position to profit by means of "way leaves"; selling the simple right to transport coal by wagonway over their property. By 1770, there were around 10 miles of operational wagonway in the area, meaning it had certainly been established and presumably in steady use for nearly 150 years with little progression or improvements deemed necessary. The system also merited and prompted wide interest, suggesting that it was a relatively scarce innovation. A French traveller and writer, Saint-Fond, who visited Newcastle, mentioned them in his book "Travels in England, Scotland, and the Hebrides" in 1791, stating he was impressed with the system, recommending its introduction to France.

By the dawn of the nineteenth century, the increasingly momentous pace of the Industrial Revolution in Britain prompted a need for more efficient transportation of goods in the sort of bulk never seen before in history. All modern advances in road and rail are duly based on this demand, and it was to the wagonways that engineers and innovators looked, eventually transforming the system to incorporate the feats of bold engineering often associated with the railway today. Yet its evolution was relatively slow, both in the chiefly anticipated way – overcoming the difficulties in advancing the required technology – but also in simply finding the willingness for a new system to be accepted by people, ideas not often travelling well.

This is best seen in the example of the "plate way", rails with iron facings applied, which was first installed at Whitehaven in Cumbria as early as 1738. That in itself was an advance of the technology – making the system more robust – but it was not until 1776 that the idea was taken further, with a true cast iron railway appearing with rails nailed to wooden sleepers. This was laid down at the Duke of Norfolk's colliery near Sheffield, designed and constructed by John Curr, and proved to be more durable and reliable; a real advance in the development of rail. What seemed like progress was, however, strongly resisted. Workers feared it would signal the end of their use and employment, reacting with such force that they rioted and actually tore the railway up. Curr was forced to take flight to a nearby wood in which he hid for three days, later deciding to abandon his scheme.

Such reactions may have played a role in delaying the advance of the cause, with inventors and entrepreneurs potentially cowed into keeping their insights to themselves; significant ideas going untapped. A period of relative inactivity followed until 1800, at which point Benjamin Outram, of Little Eaton in Derbyshire, introduced stone instead of wooden props supporting the ends and joints between rails. This practice became generally adopted, the railway slipping into common language as "Outram roads", a term which became contracted to "tram roads". Their use began to expand once again, meaning that at the turn of the nineteenth century it was, more often than not, the generally accepted method of haulage in and around mines and across the industry.

Interestingly, the railway's rise to prominence was being monitored very carefully by canal owners, including the Duke of Bridgewater, whose place in history was assured having funded the first industrial canal. He is known to have said that his enterprise would, "...do well enough if we can keep clear of these damned tram roads – there's mischief in them!" Yet as long as rail was reliant on horse power it was already at maximum efficiency, just as the canals were, meaning it would remain a robust competitor in industrial haulage rather than an overarching threat to all other forms of transport. Neither could it jeopardise employment, as manpower was still required to guide the carts – workers supervising loading and unloading as well as directing and caring for the horses. Yet the Duke obviously recognised rail's huge potential given the application of technology that inventors were already dabbling in, recognising that rail, and only rail, had the ability to cope with the massive capacity demanded by the Industrial Revolution if it could be allied to a mobile engine.

Despite British inventors and entrepreneurs being inextricably and indelibly linked with the notion of industrial progress during the period, the first person known to have suggested harnessing steam power to make an engine mobile was actually French. He was Solomon de Caus, whose championing of such a seismic industrial idea led him to suffer a bizarre and unfortunate fate. This was recorded at a time when he was housed at the Bicetre Hospital in Paris around 1641, then used as a lunatic asylum which later saw the Marquis de Sade's imprisonment, and his incarceration was noted in a letter written by Marion de Lorme, a French courtesan. She visited the asylum to find de Caus rabidly claiming his sanity to any and all who would listen: "a frightful face appeared behind some immense bars, and a hoarse voice exclaimed, 'I am not mad! I am not mad! I have made a discovery that would enrich the country that adopted it.'" In the writings, de Lorme goes on to explain how de Caus, convinced of the importance of his idea of using steam engines to power vehicles, travelled from Normandy to present the notion directly to the King Louis XIII himself, only to be refused access, dismissed by the attending Cardinal Richelieu. Far from accepting the setback, de Caus began to hound the Cardinal who, exasperated, ordered him to be sectioned at Bicetre.

In many ways, de Caus was a visionary, not least because the method used to harness the power of steam had not yet been agreed. One of the first to propose the means for a steam-driven engine was the English inventor Thomas Savery, who patented an early model in July 1698. This was a more rudimentary and generalised idea, as the original application notes, "*for raising of water and occasioning motion to all sorts of mill work by the impellent force of fire, which will be of great use and advantage for drayning mines, serveing townes with water, and for the working of all sorts of mills where they have not the benefitt of water nor constant windes.*" It was demonstrated to the Royal Society in the following year and was an important

VIADUCT ACROSS THE SANKEY VALLEY – LIVERPOOL & MANCHESTER RAILWAY

breakthrough for the age, yet it remained hampered by its reliance on atmospheric pressure, only effective when operating deep underground. It also proved to be temperamental; even when it worked, it was inefficient and in need of frequent repair. Savery's discovery spoke of mere potential, unable to be applied to transport – indeed it was never even applied to work as an effective static engine in mines for any significant period of time.

As is often the case with the development of ideas, one man rarely achieves alone. Savery's breakthrough inspired others to build on his discovery, yet successful attempts to harness steam for transport were rare during the period dating from his discovery. The notion was prominent and of deep interest to some of the keenest inventive scientists of the age, but it took the intervention of James Watt, the famous Scottish mechanical engineer, to bring the idea back from dormancy. He applied himself to the notion and built on established ideas to patent a steam engine vehicle in 1784. Having successfully installed several static steam engines to pump water from mines, mostly in Cornwall in the 1770s, he proposed a development of the technology, using it to power a slightly curious steam driven carriage capable of transporting two passengers. Watt's vehicle was never actually built, not even in prototype form, and he instead devoted the majority of his time and genius to refining the steam engine design. Yet he played his part, finally discovering the power of the condenser which radically improved the efficiency and capacity of output of steam engines and also went on to develop the notion of horsepower, with the watt unit of energy (defined as one joule per second, a measure of the rate of energy conversion or transfer) also bearing his name.

The accolade for the invention of the first known self-propelled mechanical vehicle harnessing steam power again belongs to France, fitting considering it was also home to the idea's inception. It was the brainchild of Nicolas-Joseph Cugnot, who built a prototype in 1769 and a larger model the following year, one supposedly capable of carrying four passengers and a load of four tonnes at five miles per hour, although contemporary sources state it only reached half that speed. Reports also exist of it moving with such force unexpectedly during a 1771 test that it knocked down part of a wall – technically the world's first automobile accident – at the Arsenal Museum in Paris. Where Cugnot innovated, others followed – whether by coincidence or design. Records also exist relating to an arrangement made in 1787 between the American Oliver Evans and the US state of Maryland which granted him exclusive rights to manufacture and use steam carriages yet, like so many other attempts at the time, his invention never came to any practical use or implementation. Similarly, William Symington, the Scottish engineer and inventor of the world's first practical steamboat known as the Charlotte Dundas, had adapted his design to suit a carriage. Yet his invention was also destined to fail, prevented from passing into any sort of routine use as Scotland's roads were so bad as to render any vehicle impractical, a very common problem at the time.

It was not until 1784 – the same year that Watt's idea was patented – that the first English-made, small-scale working model of a steam powered vehicle was produced. This was a small, foot high, three wheeled prototype made by William Murdoch, one of Watt's assistants. Yet it too was ill-fated, comically so. During testing one night in Cornwall on a narrow country lane leading to a church, the engine quickly outran Murdoch who, it is said, heard wails of panic coming from the darkness ahead. These came from the local priest who, confused and frightened by the sudden encounter with such strange and alien machinery, declared it to be the devil incarnate. Duly chastened, Murdoch was to take his plans no further.

All these attempts to harness steam from the latter part of the eighteenth century proved fruitless. Either inefficient or unreliable, they were destined to be looked on as dalliances by their inventors who were pushed or encouraged to apply themselves to other, more pressing, contemporary issues. The notion was almost deemed stuff of science fiction, constricted by the rather crude workings of steam engines at the time. Yet by the dawn of the nineteenth century, tramways, wagonways and horse drawn carts were becoming a common sight up and down Britain and Watt's invention of the steam engine spurred further growth which was readily adopted by heavy industry. With this, the notion that rails should be extended to effect the movement of goods to and between towns, or to where canals weren't practical, was one that began to generally percolate through the more scientific and practical industrial minds of the age. These, of course, were by no means limited to just George Stephenson as a means of effective mass transport via rails was sought, with many agreeing that the crux to the matter lay in making the steam engine mobile.

On the 11th February 1800, Mr Thomas, of Denton in Newcastle Upon Tyne, was the first to suggest the idea in a paper he presented to the Literary and Philosophical Society of Newcastle. In 1801, the same idea was suggested by Dr James Anderson in Edinburgh, who expounded beautifully on his idea, laying out his vision in saying that rail would "... widen the circle of intercourse; you form, as it were, a new creation, not only of stones and earth, and trees and plants, but of men also, and, what is more, of industry, happiness and joy. Indeed, it is scarcely possible to contemplate an institution from which would result a greater quantity of harmony, peace, and comfort, to persons living in the country, than would naturally result from the introduction of railroads." Anderson zealously advocated and envisaged a world of self-promoting prosperity, with towns and people linked for the first time across the nation. His flowing, evocative language assumes progress would be virtuous, hindsight showing this to now be a charmingly naive view considering the social and urban squalor that came hand in hand with the pressures of the Industrial Age.

The pressure mounted to find a solution to make rail travel practical. In 1802, Richard Lovell Edgeworth took the idea further, positing a system for stationary steam engines placed at regular intervals along a track to pull carriages attached to large, circulating chains. This idea never came to fruition, but it was a type of forerunner to a breakthrough he was to later find – the caterpillar track – rather than the solution to developing a mobile engine which was widely sought. Yet, in a dynamic repeated in the history of technological innovation, his idea was to stir others to action.

Richard Trevethick, a Cornish tin mine captain, was one of its chief innovators. He was determined to make steam a viable method for powering transport and turned his attention to making a carriage for use on common roads. Taking out a patent in 1802 with his cousin Andrew Vivian, the financial backer, the prototype had the outward appearance of the type of four wheeled stagecoach in common use at the time. However, was called a "Mechanical Traveller", an engine which moved on, effectively, its own legs which were designed to mimic the independent action of those as seen on a horse. Yet this ended in tragedy – it exploded during a trial, killing several bystanders.

The next important character to enter the unfolding saga was John Blekinsop, a mining engineer based in Leeds, who was the most successful of those attempting to tackle the perceived rail adhesion problem. His solution dating to 1811 was to introduce a rack and pinion rail – a wheel of his twin cylinder engine fitted with teeth which gripped to corresponding holes in the track – to counteract slippage (this rail and wheel being in addition to the normal, smooth ones). Engines based on this design began running from Middleton collieries to Leeds, a distance of roughly three and a half miles, from August 1812 and went on to achieve notable success, pulling up to 31 wagons at speeds of up to three miles per hour, becoming a local attraction to boot. However, the engine later proved to be costly and unreliable, damaging the rails as it worked on them, not distributing the weight of its load evenly.

Blekinsop's achievements attracted the attention of John Blackett, whose works at Wylam colliery, a small village around 10 miles west of Newcastle Upon Tyne, employed a wagon way thought to be one of the oldest in northern England. It ran down to Lemington on the Tyne, a distance of four miles and, in an interesting twist of fate, actually passed very close to the cottage where George Stephenson was born in 1781. It was also a painfully slow route, only allowing two journeys for a man and horse a day, a situation that Blackett was keen to improve. He therefore ordered a steam engine from Trevethick in 1812, one built by Thomas Waters in Gateshead on commission, and altered his track to incorporate the tooth and rack idea. However, it was a spectacular failure – weighing six tonnes and of a convoluted, inefficient design, it required constant attention and even broke apart during its first test on the rails. Blackett decommissioned it, but was not put off the notion of applying an engine to rails despite the commonly held belief that he was effectively throwing good money after bad. Instead, he took matters in his own hands and commissioned an engine to be made in Wylam's own workshops. Nicknamed "Black Billy", it was a qualified success. Somewhat clumsy and erratic but eminently workable, it was capable of pulling around nine wagons, yet often damaged the track and moved at a snail's pace, with frequent derailments meaning it had to be pulled back to the track by horses. Blackett faced the ridicule of locals and his peers – it is actually known that the engine ran at a loss – yet he persisted with the technology nonetheless.

There are also accounts of the engine confusing and even scaring people, just as Murdoch had found with his unfortunate run-in with the priest in Cornwall. Blackett's engine so alarmed one local at its unexpected approach during the night that it sent him reeling through a hedge and across fields, with him later stating he had met a "terrible devil on the High Street Road". Such an account today may sound far-fetched, but it is important to envisage how terrifyingly unreal the engine was at the time, especially to those unused to or even unaware of the developments in mechanical technology. Many suddenly faced with such a strange machine grinding its way along a track, emitting flames, smoke and blasts of steam would be intimidated rather than intrigued. Far from being embraced, the technology was at first shunned by the common man, viewed as a symbol of fear rather than freedom. It also frequently scared horses in the vicinity, prompting Blackett to order the engine to be stopped whenever one was near to prevent alarm. With such frequent interruptions to journeys it is understandable that his workers became annoyed and the problem counteracted much of the time saved by employing the engine.

Undeterred and unbowed by such social pressures, along with mounting financial ones, Blackett became a man who continued to experiment with technology. Crucially, he disproved the notion of slippage; the weight of a successfully operational engine conclusively shown as being more than sufficient to counteract it. At a stroke his work simplified the system, no longer demanding the sort of unnecessary adornments that Blekinsop had felt necessary to introduce.

It was only at this point that George Stephenson enters the account. Having started out with a series of menial jobs in the mining industry, in 1804 he became a Brakesman – a manual labouring position where he controlled winding gear at the pit – at Killingworth, north of Newcastle Upon Tyne. He then experienced a period of personal difficulties. In 1806, the tragic loss of his young wife Frances to tuberculosis prompted a move to Scotland which ended when his father was blinded in a mining accident a few months later. Having returned to Killingworth, he was later promoted to the position of Enginewright in 1811, having shown considerable mechanical knowledge and initiative when fixing a malfunctioning engine. An ambitious young engineer, he was determined to find a more efficient solution to the problem of mass movement of coal from Killingworth's mines to river transport on the Tyne in his new role. He recognised that he first had to become educated to achieve this goal. It is now difficult to imagine, but one of Britain's foremost engineering minds was actually illiterate until the age of 18, when he paid to study at night school, learning reading, writing and arithmetic.

The high price of corn at the time meant keeping horses, the resource on which all haulage depended, was relatively expensive. A more permanent and economical solution to transport issues was becoming an increasingly pressing need as the volume of coal being transported steadily increased. Stephenson became fixated on the notion of a "travelling engine", as they were known, and began the search for a way to apply one to rail. He studied Blackett's engines at Wylam and inspected Trevethick's "Black Billy" and the plateway on which it ran. He was an effervescent and bullish character and, having made his appraisals of his peers' work, he found them – quite fairly, it must be said – to be clumsy, unsophisticated machines with crowded designs. He was certain he could make major improvements. He also remained resolutely upbeat with regard to the technology's capabilities, believing in the potential power of the invention. This flew in the face of the accepted opinion – many at the time saw the steam engine as a dalliance, little more than an expensive toy. Stephenson was also a realist, recognising that the achievements of engines at the dawn of the nineteenth century amounted to nothing more than a simple, unreliable substitution for horse power. He devoted his full attention to exploring the technology, setting his sights on incremental improvements rather than wholesale breakthroughs.

Stephenson was fortunate in having the backing of Lord

Ravensworth at Killingworth. A stout financier, he provided the required capital needed to invest in the steam engine project. Yet such backing was not a panacea. Stephenson still found it tricky to source a team of mechanics skilful enough to follow his instructions and ideas, most being located in the industrial hubs of London, Birmingham and Manchester, their skills in demand in such expanding urban centres. Provision of tools was also lacking and the facilities at Killingworth were somewhat crude, with Stephenson having to largely make do with what was at hand in terms of equipment, materials and personnel. He often taught the men himself.

The first wrought iron locomotive that Stephenson produced in 1814 bore the hallmarks of such trying circumstances. It followed Blekinsop's blueprint and took ten months to complete. The final engine had no springs, being simply mounted on a wooden frame on the rail, with the weight of the engine providing the traction to counteract the idea of slippage. It became popularly known as "The Bultcher" and was still rough around the edges: crowded in terms of design, over-reliant on the boiler to generate power and used as a basis for the fixings. Energy was transmitted to the wheels unevenly, leading to a jerky, rattling motion. Despite this, it still proved to be the most successful working engine ever constructed when it entered service on the 25th of July, pulling eight carriages of 30 tonnes at four miles per hour. Yet its biggest drawback was that, crucially, it was no more economical than regular horsepower – its speed the same as an average horse's walking pace.

Displaying typical tenacity in applying himself to his calling in dedicated fashion, despite modest, initial success that might have lead others to become complacent, Stephenson went back to the drawing board. This was crucial, as in refining his design he made a major breakthrough. He discovered that steam previously allowed to simply escape into the atmosphere could be redirected back into the chimney, an innovation known as the steam blast. This could effectively double the power of the engine as the increased airflow heightened the draught in the furnace, keeping the level of combustion at the fiercest level possible. The modern, far more powerful and efficient engine would have been an impossible proposition without it. In many ways, Stephenson's discovery was the turning point in the modern transport revolution.

Bolstered by his discovery, Stephenson set about building a new engine to include it, also incorporating a total redesign of the layout of the components and mechanics of the locomotive. His new design was registered in a patent on the 28th of February 1815. Among the revisions, he chose to communicate kinetic energy more efficiently by linking the cylinders and the wheels of the engine directly. His use of a "ball and socket" joint to do this ensured that the wheels made constant contact with the rails despite any irregularities in the groundwork along the track's route, unevenness having frequently derailed previous engines. The wheels were also arranged to work in pairs, therefore keeping a constant pace in relation to one another, leading to a smoother ride and increased efficiency. Stephenson designed a much more powerful engine that wasted much less energy.

Further improvements were made in 1816. At this point, Stephenson instead set his sights on the efficiency of the rail, citing it as being as crucial in the overall efficiency of travel as the engine. He uniquely took this position during a period where the focus was almost always on improving the workings of the locomotive. Rails were all too often an afterthought, laid haphazardly which led to inevitable problems, although they were not necessarily recognised as causing them. For example, as tracks were rarely levelled end to end, there was inevitable wear and tear to the engine as it banged along, with poor general maintenance leading to further problems, even derailments. To counteract this, Stephenson invented a new means of fixing rails in place which prevented the points between them being prone to subsidence, and in also curving the joint of one rail over the next he introduced a much smoother plane for an engine to travel on. These improved rails were successfully launched at Killingworth and are noted in a patent, named jointly with William Losh, a wealthy iron manufacturer who also backed Stephenson financially, lodged on the 30th of September 1816. It is listed as being "for their invented new method or methods of facilitating the conveyance of carriages, and all manner of goods and materials along railways and tramways."

A lasting testament to Stephenson's engineering prowess can also be seen in the way he used his initiative, applying his flair with mechanics even when facing a problem that had not been tackled before. This was most clear when revising his engine design. He felt that the durability of the springs which supported the engine needed great improvement, but was hamstrung in his efforts to have suitable ones built. The type of steel springs with strength and durability required simply didn't exist, with only a handful of people with the ability to produce something suitable working in Britain at the time. Stephenson was therefore forced to improvise, and did so brilliantly. He instead rerouted steam to do the job for him, connecting the upper side of the axles to the boiler via cylinders containing floating pistons, the rods of which distributed the pressure from the boiler and weight of the engine equally across the wheels. Stephenson essentially, and seemingly effortlessly, invented steam springs until the technology existed to have steel ones in their place.

This was among a raft of improvements that Stephenson introduced overall, making steam engines increasingly reliable and economical to run and taking their efficiency well beyond that of horses. His successes and increasingly prestigious profile tempted him to focus on making the steam engine mobile on common roads, with the general expectation being that he was capable of surpassing Trevethick's work. It was an issue that certainly captured Stephenson's imagination. In October 1818 he laid the groundwork for pursuing the notion, conducting a series of trials using a device he invented – a dynamometer – to measure the forces at work on an engine in motion. These experiments proved that friction was a constant at all velocities, confirming a long-held theory that had not been proven in any practical test before. He even highlighted the impact on different engine components: the axles, the outside surfaces of the wheel and the rail, measuring the level of friction and impact of gravity with some accuracy. He was, however, less able to work out the resistance acting on wheels on a road. Without a prototype to test on common roads, Stephenson instead sprinkled sand on rails. Having observed the laboured motion of the engine on a moderately uneven surface, he decided that the idea was simply not worth pursuing given the state of Britain's roads at the time. He therefore continued to focus fully on the potential of rail.

Stephenson used these tests to found a key axiom of rail travel, as they helped him determine that a flat, level track was

RAINHILL BRIDGE ON THE LIVERPOOL & MANCHESTER RAILWAY

73

ENTRANCE TO THE TUNNEL OF THE LIVERPOOL & MANCHESTER RAILWAY, EDGE HILL

RAILWAYS IN OPERATION
1836

The year 1836 was the last year but one of the reign of William IV (Queen Victoria succeeded to the throne in 1837), and the head of the Government was Lord Melbourne. England was then in the throes of political and social revolution. Improved methods of agriculture had lead to the enclosure of land by the great land owners and the disappearance of the village yeoman, who became landless labourer's drifting to the towns for employment. The nation witnessed industrialization proceeding at a rapid pace, and the social problems it would create, urban housing, working conditions, public health and public order to name but a few. Pressure to extend the franchise to the middle classes had led to the Reform Act, 1832, but when the working class realized that they had gained nothing from the Act, they sought to express their indignation in revolutionary ways. In 1834 the Grand National Consolidated Trades Union of Great Britain and Ireland (GNCTU) was established and in 1836 a group of working-class men held a meeting in London and founded the London Working Men's Association, the origin of Chartism.

The Municipal Corporation Act, 1835, was the major work of reform in the Melbourne Ministry, and swept away many anomalies in local government administration. The Metropolitan Police had already been established in 1829, and an Act of 1835 led to the overhaul of police arrangements in the boroughs.

Against this background the railways had their beginning; the essence of the railway revolution lay in the development of steam, as demonstrated by Stephenson in 1815. Initially, the railways met with fierce opposition. Stage-coach proprietors, inn-keepers and horse dealers saw their livelihoods jeopardized and the canal companies feared the new competition. However, the natural conservatism of the country was the most potent opposition, and trains were condemned as "dangerous and a nuisance". This resistance enormously increased the cost of starting new lines and it had been reckoned that the cost of surveying the ground and getting a Bill through Parliament amounted to an average of £4,000 per mile of track laid. It was then necessary to buy the land, and the land owners being opposed to the scheme demanded exorbitant prices. In the case of the Great Western line, for example, the cost was £6,696 per mile, the nature of the English countryside was still another factor in the heavy cost of railways, especially in the west and north where so many tunnels, viaducts and bridges were needed. But in spite of these set-backs, the money was forthcoming and by 1855 no less than £300 million had been invested. Most of this money was private capital.

Initially the railways were financed by local people, interested in their own local railway, but, when the high profits of the Liverpool-Manchester Railway became known, promoters became active all over the country and anyone with money to invest was welcomed. The years 1836-1837 have indeed been referred to as the "little railway mania", to distinguish it from the real mania of the 1840's.

The railways in this country were thus a field for the small investor and entirely dependent on private enterprise. While in France and Germany the railways were planned as national enterprises, in England the principal of laissez-faire was too well established, and although a series of Government Committees considered the question of a national railway policy, only one, Gladstone's Committee of 1844 recommended a gradual taking over of railways by the State.

The men responsible for building the railways, navigators or navvies as they were called created a social problem in themselves. Hardworking and hard-living, they descended in large numbers on the countryside, and the difficulties of finding food and accommodation were enormous. The roughest accommodation usually had to suffice and food was frequently obtained from a "tommy shop" run by the contractor or one of the gangers. Isolated from the community by their rude life, they tended to create a world of their own, and sought relaxation from their dangerous work in orgies of drinking and violence. Fond of display in their velvet trousers and bright plush waistcoats, violent, intemperate, conceited and vicious, they were never the less fearless and loyal. If the Railway Police owes its origin to their extravagances, it was they who under almost impossible conditions of exposure and danger laid down the framework of the railways as we know them today.

1. Newcastle and Carlisle Railway

Company formed 1829.
Opened in stages from 1835 to 1839.
Originally intended to be drawn by horsepower, but locomotives substituted.
Absorbed by N.E Railway in 1862.

2. Stanhope and Tyne Railway

Company formed in 1831.
Intended to connect the limekilns of Stanhope and collieries of Medomsley with South Shields for shipments.
Line opened 1834.
Reconstructed after financial difficulties in 1841 and the northern portion taken over by the Pontop and South Shields Railway in 1842.

BUILDING RETAINING WALL NEAR PARK STREET, CAMDEN TOWN – LONDON TO BIRMINGHAM RAILWAY SEPT 17TH 1836

RAILWAYS IN OPERATION
1839

The next map in our History of the Railways in Maps is dated 1839, the second year in the reign of Queen Victoria, this year saw a Cabinet crisis generally referred to as the Bedchamber Question. It arose when Lord Melbourne's Whig Ministry resigned and Sir Robert Peel formed a Tory one. Sir Robert then advised the Queen that the Whig Ladies of the Bedchamber were not acceptable to a Tory Government and should be replaced by Tory Ladies. The Queen objected and gained her point, where-upon Peel refused the Government and Melbourne formed his third ministry.

The Chartist agitation had by 1839 gained considerable momentum, the movement's newspaper, entitled The Northern Star, and selling at 4½d. per copy, had reached a circulation of 24,000. Demonstrations were inevitable and riots occurred at Birmingham and elsewhere. At a riot in Newport, the crowd was fired on by Constables and no less than 20 persons were killed. John Frost, the leader, and others were sentenced to death, but were ultimately transported.

It was in 1839 that Rowland Hill decided to introduce the Penny Postage, though the scheme did not get under way until early in 1840.

In the field of science and engineering this was the year when Kirkpatrick MacMillan of Dumfries invented the first real bicycle, and Charles Goodyear, an American, discovered vulcanized rubber by accident. Moritz Jacobi's rotary motor invented in 1834, was successfully introduced in a boat carrying fourteen passengers, and the Peninsula and Oriental Line (P. & O.) established a steamship service from England to Alexandria which met ships of the East India Company coming up the Red Sea.

In Railway Affairs, a Select Committee was formed in April 1839, 'to enquire into the state of communication by railways' and in second report of that year it dealt with the following three points: (1) the financial position of the companies and the methods of dealing in shares, (2) various points in the actual operation of railways, (3) the incidence of the Government tax of 1/8 d. per mile leviable on all passengers, irrespective of class.

The 1839 reports of this Committee, together with those of the following year, resulted in a Bill for regulating railways being introduced into The House of Commons during 1840, and this measure ultimately became law. This Act became especially important as marking the first stage in State Control of our railways.

1. Newcastle and Carlisle Railway

(*See* 2 – **Map 1836**)

2. Newcastle and North Shields Railway

Company formed in 1836.
Line opened 1839.

3. The Brandling Junction Railway

Company formed in 1835.
The object of this railway was to connect Gateshead with South Shields and Sunderland. An interesting feature is that the Enabling Act was obtained by a private person, a Mr. R. W. Brandling, who subsequently disposed of his rights to a private company.
The first portion of the line, an extension from the Newcastle and Carlisle line at Redheugh, through Gateshead to Hilgate Wharf, was opened in January, 1839. The second section from High Shields to Monkwearmouth, was opened in June, 1839, to be followed in August, 1839, by the Gateshead to Harton portion and the Wearmouth dock branch.
The railway was purchased in 1844 by the Newcastle and Darlington Junction Company, though purchase was not legalised until an Act of 1845.

4. Pontop and South Shields Railway

(*See* 2 – **Map 1836**)
Formerly the Stanhope and Tyne Railway.

5. Durham and Sunderland Railway

(*See* 3 – **Map 1836**).

6. Durham Junction Railway

Company formed in 1834.
Originally intended to extend from a junction with the Stanhope and Tyne Railway at Washington to the northern terminus of the Hartlepool Railway at Moorsley, it was never constructed beyond Rainton. Nevertheless it formed an indispensible link in the East Coast route between London and Scotland.
The line was opened for mineral traffic in 1838, and for passenger traffic in 1840.
In 1843 it was purchased by the Newcastle and Darlington Junction Company and later became part of the North Eastern system.

7. Hartlepool Dock Railway

(*See* 4 – **Map 1836**)

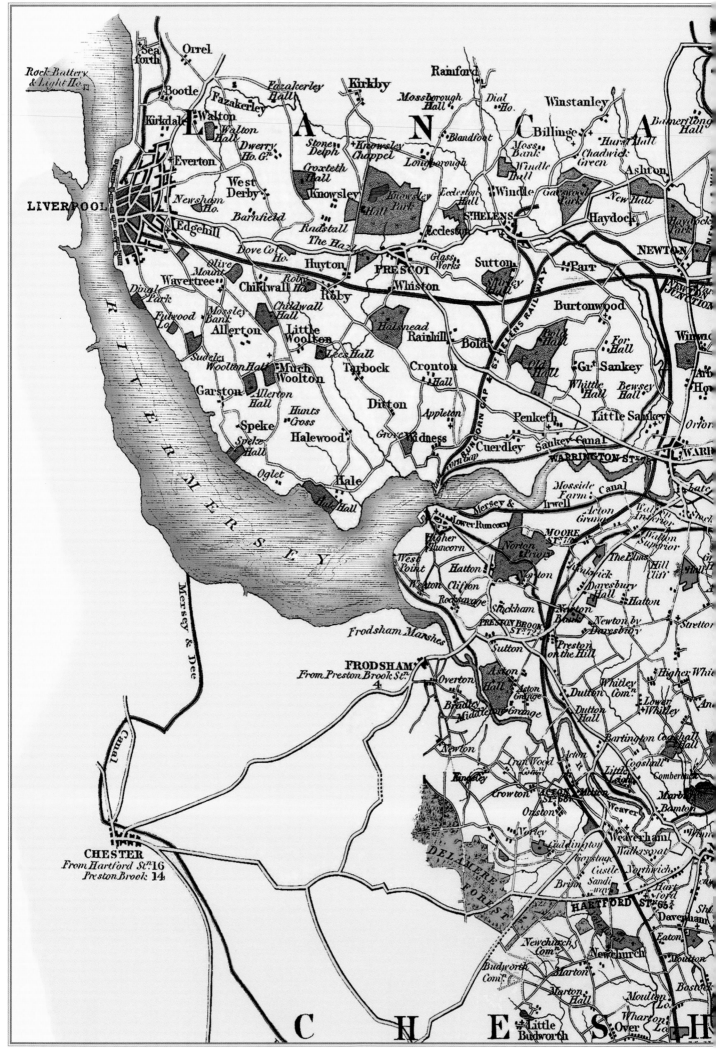

NORTHERN SECTION OF OSBORNES MAP OF THE GRAND JUNCTION

8. Clarence Railway

(*See* 5 – **Map 1836**)

9. Stockton and Darlington Railway

(*See* 6 – **Map 1836**)

10. Whitby and Pickering Railway

(*See* 7 – **Map 1836**)

11. York and North Midland Railway

Company formed in 1836.
Originally intended to connect York with the North Midlands at Normanton. The first of its short branches connected York with the Leeds and Selby Railway at South Milford, a distance of 14½ miles and this was opened in 1839. It is this branch which is shown on this map. It was in connection with the York and North Midland that George Hudson first came into prominence.

12. Leeds and Selby Railway

(*See* 8 – **Map 1836**)

13. Preston and Wigan Railway
(North Union Railway)

Company formed in 1837.
This was in effect an extension of the Wigan Branch Railway (*See* 12 – **Map 1836**) to Preston.
It was not until 1834 when the two lines were amalgamated under the title of the North Union Railway that construction began.
This was the first railway amalgamation with Parliamentary sanction.
The line was opened in 1838, thus completing a chain over four companies' lines from Euston to Preston, a total of 218 miles.
In 1844 the North Union amalgamated with the Bolton and Preston under its former name.
The North Union Railway was leased to the London and North Western and Lancashire and Yorkshire Railways from 1846.

14. Liverpool and Manchester Railway

(*See* 9 – **Map 1836**)

15. St. Helens and Runcorn Railway

(*See* 10 – **Map 1836**)

16. Warrington and Newton Railway

(*See* 11 – **Map 1836**)

17. Wigan Branch Railway

(*See* 12 – **Map 1836**)

18. Bolton and Leigh Railway

(*See* 13 – **Map 1836**)

19. Leigh and Kenyon Railway

(*See* 14 – **Map 1836**)

20. Manchester and Bolton Railway

Company formed in 1831.
This was the outcome of a scheme to convert the existing canal of the Manchester, Bolton and Bury Navigation Company into a railway, but it was subsequently decided to build the railway parallel to the canal. It extended from Salford to Bolton and was about 10 miles long.
The line was opened in 1838 to passenger and freight services.
In 1846 the Company amalgamated with Manchester and Leeds Railway and the line later became part of the London-Midland system.

21. Manchester-Leeds Railway

Company formed in 1836.
This was intended, with other lines, to connect the principal commercial ports of the east and west coasts. It was to extend from a terminus at Oldham Road, Manchester, to a junction with the North Midland at Normanton, and pass by the towns of Rochdale, Todmorden and Wakefield.
The first section from Manchester to the south end of the long tunnel through the Pennines at Littleborough was opened in 1839.

22. Sheffield and Rotherham Railway

Company formed in 1836.
This was a short but important line from Wicker (the long standing principal goods station in Sheffield) to Rotherham, 5½ miles away, with a branch line of 1½ miles to the Greasborough Canal, and thence, by a connection, to the North Midland Railway.
The line to Rotherham was opened in 1838 and the Greasborough branch in 1839.

23. Grand Junction Railway

Company formed in 1833.
The original scheme was to connect Birmingham with Birkenhead, but ultimately it was decided to carry the line to Warrington and there to join the Warrington and Newton Railway (*See* 11 – **Map 1836**), so linking Birmingham with Liverpool.
It proved a much easier line to construct than the London to Birmingham, having no tunnel, and was opened throughout its length in 1837.
From this date through passenger trains were run via Newton Junction between Birmingham, Liverpool and Manchester.

24. Midland Counties Railway

Company formed in 1836.
Originally intended to recover Derbyshire's coal trade with Leicester which had been lost with the opening of the Leicester and Swannington Railway.
The scheme as eventually approved by Parliament involved a main line of 50 miles from Derby to Rugby with a branch line of 7 miles from Trent to Nottingham.
The first 16 miles of the line, from Derby to Nottingham, were opened in1839.

25. Birmingham and Derby Junction Railway

Company formed in 1836.
Intended to connect a junction with the North Midland and Midland Counties Railway at Derby with the London and Birmingham Railway at Stetchford, just outside Birmingham.
Owing to friction between North Midland and Midland Counties Railways, because the North Midland Company feared that an extension of the Midland Counties would interfere with their traffic, the Birmingham and Derby Company was induced to add a branch of 6½ miles from Whitacre to Hampton (on the London and Birmingham) to their scheme.
The line was opened in 1839.

26. Leicester and Swannington

(*See* 15 – **Map 1836**)

27. London and Birmingham Railway

Company formed in 1833.
Two projects for a railway between London and Birmingham were mooted as early as 1825, one via Coventry, the other via Oxford, but it was not until 1831 that a bill for a railway via Coventry was ready for presentation to Parliament. This scheme was recommended by George and Robert Stephenson who had been appointed joint engineers. The line was to extend from Camden Town to Grosvenor Row in Birmingham, approximately 111 miles.
In 1835, a supplementary Act authorized the extension of 1¼ miles from Camden Town to Euston Square. Initially trains had to be hauled up this gradient of 1 in 70 by endless rope and fixed engine! But in 1844 this system was superseded by ordinary locomotives whose performance had meanwhile improved.
The first section of the London and Birmingham was opened in July, 1837, from Euston to Boxmoor, a further section to Tring being completed by October. Tunnels at Primrose Hill, Watford, and Kilsby delayed progress, but the line was finally opened throughout in 1838. This led to a reduction in the travelling time from London to Preston from 18 hours to 11 hours, with a consequent acceleration of mails to Edingburgh and Glasgow.

28. Aylesbury Railway

Company formed in 1836.
This was a branch railway of 7 miles only, connecting Aylesbury with the London and Birmingham Railway at Cheddington.
It was opened in 1838.

THE VIADUCT OVER THE MERSEY AND THE MERSEY & IRWELL CANAL ON THE GRAND JUNCTION RAILWAY

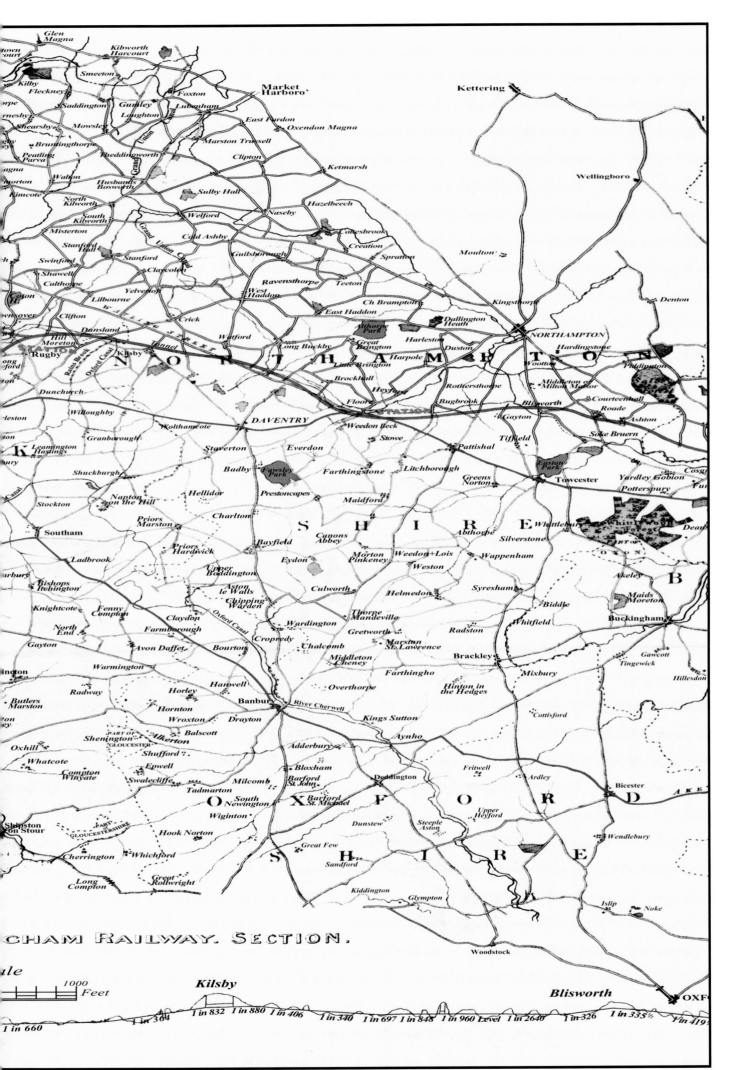

FREELINGS MAP OF LONDON & BIRMINGHAM RAILWAY

Map 1842

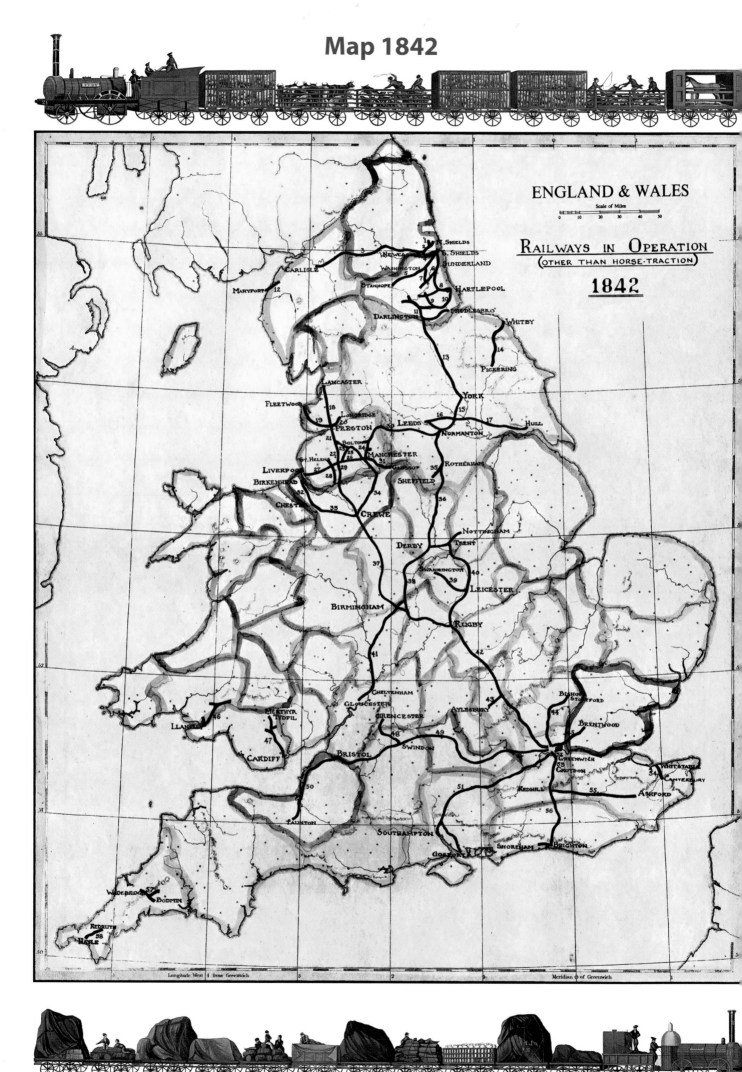

ENGLAND & WALES

Scale of Miles

0 10 20 30 40 50

RAILWAYS IN OPERATION
(OTHER THAN HORSE-TRACTION)

1842

RAILWAYS IN OPERATION
1842

We now have reached 1842, the fifth year of Queen Victoria's reign and the second year of the ministry of Sir Robert Peel who took office in 1841. Quite apart from the increasing momentum of railway construction there had been a vast development of the coal trade which contributed to the prevailing national prosperity. It has been estimated that about 118,000 were employed in the mines at this time. Working conditions in the mines had, however, been deplorable and following the report of the Children's Employment Commission, which reported to Parliament in 1842 of the extensive employment of women and children below ground, Ashley's Act, was passed prohibiting the employment of women and girls entirely and all boys under 10 years old.

Meanwhile the Chartist agitation was still in progress. The National Chartist Association was pursuing its work of securing signatures for the second Charter Petition. It was said that more than three million people signed it.

The procession which bore it to the House of Commons stretched from Westminster to Oxford Circus, but the petition was rejected by the Commons and strikes then occurred in Stalybridge and spread to Manchester, through Lincolnshire, and Yorkshire, Staffordshire, Warwickshire and Wales. Riots occurred in several manufacturing districts, but irresolution and disagreement rent the ranks of the Chartists and the strike began to fail. Many arrests were made and eventually the movement collapsed.

Two attacks upon the Queen's person occurred in 1842. On the 29th May, as the Queen and Prince Albert were returning to Buckingham Palace, down Constitution Hill in a carriage and four, John Francis, the son of a stage carpenter at Covent Garden Theatre, drew a pistol and fired at them. The Queen was untouched, but Prince Albert observed the would-be assassin and pointed him out to observers. One of the Queen's equerries then called a policeman who arrested him. A Privy Council twice examined the accused and committed him to Newgate for trial. He was eventually found guilty by the jury and Chief Justice Tindall sentenced him to be hanged, drawn and quartered, but the sentence was subsequently commuted to transportation for life.

The second attempt upon the Queen's life was made on 3rd July, by a young offender named Bean who was eventually sentenced to 18 months' imprisonment. These attacks upon the Queen aroused government concern and resulted in an extension of the law of treason by the Treason Act, 1842.

Abroad, the year 1842 is important for the termination of serious differences between the United States of America and Great Britain by the Ashburton Treaty. It also saw the end of the first Afghan War (1839-42). Anglo-Russian rivalry and suspicion lay at the root of this conflict. Russian attempts to absorb Afganistan had led, in 1839, to the occupation of Kabul by British-Indian troops led by Sir John Keane. In 1841, the Afghans, deeply resenting the loss of their independence, had murdered the British envoys, Sir William MacNaughton and Sir Alexander Burnes, and the British had signed a convention under which they were to give hostages, pay an indemnity, surrender their guns and evacuate the country. On the 6th January, 1842, 4,500 British-Indian troops with 12,000 camp followers began their retreat, but Sirdar Akbar Khan, son of Dost Mohammed, who had promised supplies and safe conduct, attacked the troops on their march and there was only one survivor. The British were determined to retrieve the disaster and dispatched fresh forces on the 16th April, 1842 and in September 1842 Kabul was recaptured by British forces.

In the Far East, the treaty of Nanking ended the war with China. Five Ports were opened to English merchants and Hong Cong was ceded to England.

In the field of science and engineering, Robert Mayor discovered the law of the conservation of energy, James Nasmyth invented the steam hammer, and W. H. Phillips built the first helicopter which was lifted a few feet off the ground by steam power.

In the world of letters, Macauley published his Lays of Ancient Rome.

1. Seghill to Percy Main

No Act was obtained for the incorporation or construction of this railway.

This was a local mineral line of 5¼ miles which was opened in June, 1840. Passenger traffic was not conveyed until August, 1841. Subsequently it was incorporated in the Blythe and Tyne Railway.

2. Newcastle and North Sheilds Railway

(*See* 2 – **Map 1839**)

3. Newcastle and Carlisle Railway

(*See* 1 – **Map 1836**)

4. Brandling Junction Railway

(*See* 3 – **Map 1839**)

THE VIADUCT AT STOCKPORT ON THE MANCHESTER & BIRMINGHAM RAILWAY

5. Pontop and South Shields Railway

(*See* 4 – **Map 1839**)

6. Durham and Sunderland Railway

(*See* 3 – **Map 1836**)

7. Durham Junction Railway

(*See* 6 – **Map 1839**)

8. Hartlepool Dock Railway

(*See* 4 – **Map 1836**)

9. Clarence Railway

(*See* 5 – **Map 1836**)

10. Stockton and Hartlepool Railway

No Act was obtained for the incorporation or construction of this railway.
This was a local line of 8 miles. Originally intended as an extension for mineral traffic of the Clarence Railway, it was opened for goods traffic in 1840 and passenger traffic in February, 1841.

11. Stockton and Darlington Railway

(*See* 6 – **Map 1836**)

12. Maryport and Carlisle Railway

Company formed in 1837.
Intended to serve part of the Cumberland coalfields.
Made a humble beginning in July, 1840 when 7 miles were opened. A further 1¼ to Aspatria was completed in 1841.

13. Great North of England Railway

Company formed in 1836.

Intended to connect Newcastle (or rather Gateshead, as the bridging of the Tyne had not then been attempted) with York.

In 1836, the Company secured Parliamentary sanction for the northern portion (34½ miles) from Gateshead to the river Tees at Croft. In 1837, The Company obtained powers to construct the southern half which met the northern half at Croft. In 1837, the Company obtained powers to construct the northern half at Croft and continued south-east for 41½ miles to a junction with the York and North Midland outside York.

The southern half of the project was opened in 1841, but the northern portion was never completed as originally intended. The Great North of England Railway Company ultimately transferred to a new company, the Newcastle and Darlington Junction (or Northern Union) Railway, incorporated 1842, their powers to complete the northern portion between Shincliffe and Newcastle.

14. Whitby and Pickering Railway

(*See* 7 – **Map 1836**)

15. York and North Midland Railway

(*See* 11 – **Map 1839**)

16. Leeds and Selby Railway

(*See* 8 – **Map 1836**)

17. Hull and Selby Railway

Company formed in 1836.

Scheme for connecting the principal commercial ports of the east and west coasts. The company pursued an almost straight and level course along the north side of the river Humber for 30¾ miles.

It was opened in the year 1840.

18. Lancaster and Preston Railway

Company formed in 1837.

The main chain of railway communications was carried 20½ miles farther north when this line was opened in June 1840.

It later formed an integral part of an improved communication with Scotland. The extension from Preston to Lancaster enabled passengers from London to the North to accomplish the journey of 238½ miles in a through carriage in 11 hours, whereas only four years earlier the whole journey had to be done by coach taking 26 hours. Because of disputes with neighbouring companies for the use of the Preston Station, the company had to make a temporary station about 200 yards north of the one in use. Passengers were compelled to walk over the intervening distance or pay 6d. each to the Northern Union Company for conveyance in a through carriage.

19. Preston and Wyre Railway

Company formed in 1835.

The need for an additional port for the manufacturers of North Lancashire was the precipice for this undertaking. It consisted of a harbor at the mouth of the river Wyre with 19½ miles of railway to connect it with Preston. Its principal promoter was a local landowner, Sir Hesketh Fleetwood, who gave his name to the port.

SHERBOURNE VIADUCT NEAR COVENTRY ON THE LONDON & BIRMINGHAM RAILWAY

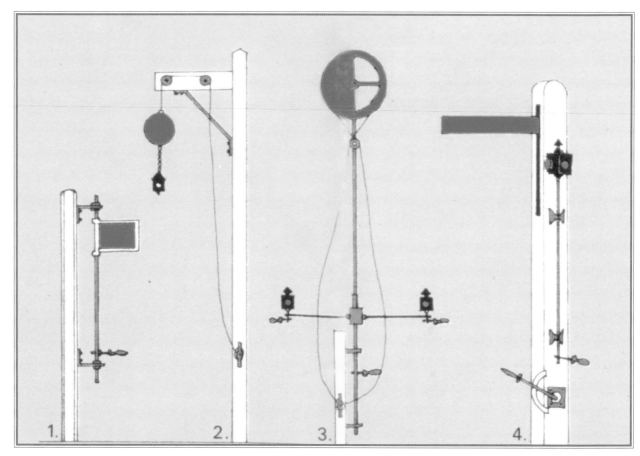

1. One of the earliest fixed signals consisting of a red flag stretched on a frame (about 1834). 2. Another early signal (about 1837) in which the ball, or lantern at night, was lowered to indicate 'danger'. 3. A more complicated signal to control two lines of traffic. The disc was rotated like a wheel, the solid side indicating danger and the cut-out side 'clear' (about 1870). 4.Slotted-post semaphore signal (about 1869). It indicated 'stop' when horizontal, 'cation' when at an angle of 45" and clear when out of sight inside slotted post.

Opened in July 1840, the line was unsuccessful for some years, in spite of extensions to Lytham and Blackpool. In 1849, it was loaned and worked jointly by the London and North Western and Lancashire and Yorkshire Companies and finally absorbed by them in 1888.

20. Preston and Longridge Railway

Company formed in 1836.
A local line of 7 miles, first intended to be worked by horse-power for bringing the produce of the various quarries in the neighbourhood of Longridge to Preston.
Opened in May, 1840, for freight traffic only.

21. Preston and Wigan Railway (North Union Railway)

(See 13 – **Map 1839**)

22. Wigan Branch Railway (North Union Railway)

(See 12 – **Map 1836**)

23. Bolton and Preston Railway

Company formed in 1837.
It soon came into violent competition with the North Union until the two companies were amalgamated in 1844.

24. Manchester and Bolton Railway

(See 20 – **Map 1839**)

25. Bolton and Leigh

(See 13 – **Map 1836**)

26. Leigh and Kenyon Railway

(See 14 – **Map 1836**)

27. Liverpool and Manchester Railway

(See 9 – **Map 1836**)

28. St. Helens and Runcorn Gap Railway

(See 10 – **Map 1836**)

29. Warrington and Newton Railway

(See 11 – **Map 1836**)

30. Manchester and Leeds Railway

(See 21 – **Map 1839**)

RAILWAYS IN OPERATION
1845

We have now reached the eighth year of Queen Victoria's reign and the fifth year of Sir Robert Peel's Ministry. This was the year in which the Anti-Corn Law Agitation began. The movement which was centered in Manchester and fostered by leaders of the Manchester School of political economists – notably Cobden and Bright – gradually captured the interest of the working class. The objects of the agitators were twofold – to secure grain imports free of tax and to establish free trade in general. An Anti-Corn Law League had been formed in 1839, but it was opposed by conservative landlords for whom the Corn Laws meant higher prices and rents.

In the world of letters, 1845 saw the appearance of Disreali's famous political novel "Sybil", Edgar Alan Poe's "Tales of Mystery" and Dumas's "Count of Monte Cristo".

It was in this year that the explorer Sir John Franklin set out in the ships Erebus and Terror to seek a north-west passage by way of Lancaster Sound in the Arctic Circle. The two vessels were sighted in Baffin Bay but no further news having been received from Franklin by 1847, no less than thirty-nine expeditions were sent from Great Britain and America in search of him. It was not until 1857 that a cairn was found at Point Victory with a record of the expedition down to 25th April, 1848, and proof that Franklin had discovered the north-west passage and had died on 11th June, 1847.

In the transport industry, 1845 is significant for the first crossing of the Atlantic by an iron vessel.

1. Seghill to Percy Main

(*See* 1 – **Map 1842**)

2. Newcastle and North Shields Railway

(*See* 2 – **Map 1839**)

3. Newcastle and Carlisle Railway

(*See* 1 – **Map 1836**)

4. Maryport and Carlisle Railway

(*See* 12 – **Map 1842**)

A section of 11¼ miles from Carlisle to Wigton was opened in May, 1843, and the line was finally completed with the opening of the remaining section from Wigton to Aspatria in February, 1845.

5. Brandling Junction Railway

(*See* 3 – **Map 1839**)

6. Pontop and South Shields Railway

(*See* 4 – **Map 1839**)

7. Durham and Sunderland Railway

(*See* 3 – **Map 1836**)

8. Durham Junction Railway

(*See* 6 – **Map 1839**)

9. Hartlepool Dock Railway

(*See* 4 – **Map 1836**)

10. Newcastle and Darlington Junction Railway

Company formed in 1842.

Intended to complete the chain of railways, as far as Gateshead. The main portion of 21¼ miles from Belmont Junction to Darlington was opened in June, 1844, and on the 18th June, 1844, a special train ran from Euston to Gateshead in eight hours and eleven minutes. It was worked from the outset by the Great North of England who provided both power and stock. In June, 1843, they bought the Durham Junction Railway to form a part of the Company's route from Darlington to Gateshead. In 1845 they also purchased the Brandling Junction Railway (See 5 above).

11. Stockton and Darlington Railway

(*See* 6 – **Map 1836**)

An extension to Crook was opened in 1844 and a further extension from Crook to Cold Rowley, primarily a mineral line, was opened in May, 1845.

12. Clarence Railway

(*See* 5 – **Map 1836**)

13. Stockton and Hartlepool Railway

(*See* 10 – **Map 1842**)

14. Great North of England Railway

(*See* 13 – **Map 1842**)

15. Whitby and Pickering Railway

(*See* 7 – **Map 1836**)

CANAL BRIDGE, PITSTONE BUCKINGHAMSHIRE – LONDON & BIRMINGHAM RAILWAY

NEW SIGNALS – JUNCTION OF THE GREAT WESTERN RAILWAY AND WEST LONDON BRANCH

45. Yarmouth and Norwich Railway
(Norfolk Railway)

Company formed in 1842.

With the curtailment of the original scheme of the Eastern Counties Railway, their compulsory powers for the purchase of land having expired in July, 1840, the inhabitants of Norfolk took matters into their own hands and obtained powers to make a line of 20½ miles to connect the capital of the county with its chief port.

The completed line was opened throughout in April, 1844, with intermediate stations at Reedham, Cantley, Buckenham and Brundall.

46. Norwich and Brandon Railway
(Norfolk Railway)

Company formed in 1844.

This constituted of a line of 35 miles and a branch of 3¼ miles to Thetford and was part of the plan to connect up Norwich and Yarmouth with the main railway system, consequent on the failure of the Eastern Counties Railway to carry out its original proposals.

The line was opened in July, 1845, when the company and the Yarmouth and Norwich Railway agreed to amalgamate on equal terms, the combined companies being named the Norfolk Railway.

47. Eastern Counties Railway

(See 30 – **Map 1839** and 44 – **Map 1842**)

Eastern England presented the best ground for railway development, chiefly because of the favorable nature of the country for railway construction. This enabled lines to be speedily and economically constructed. A remarkable instance of this is the Eastern Counties line – 56 miles – from Bishops Stortford to Brandon. Although an Act had been obtained for the 10 miles section from Bishops Stortford to Newport in 1843, an Act had not been obtained for the construction of the remaining 46 miles until July, 1844, and yet the completed line was opened a year later, in July, 1845.

48. Great Western Railway

(See 29 – **Map 1839** and 48 – **Map 1842**)

The Oxford Branch to Didcot, originally incorporated as the Oxford Branch Railway in 1843 and absorbed later by the Great Western was opened in June, 1844.

The section from Kemble to Stonehouse (Standish Junction) was opened in May, 1845.

49. Bristol and Gloucester Railway

Company formed in 1828.

Although originally intended as a railway between Bristol and Gloucester, the scheme was whittled down by its Act to a line of 9 miles in length extending from Bristol to the collieries near Westerleigh. This was constructed as a horse railway and was opened in August, 1835. In 1839 the original intention matured and an Act was obtained to extend the line for 22¼ miles to a junction with the Cheltenham and Great Western Union (Great Western Railway) at Standish. The extension was completed and the whole line opened as a locomotive railway in July, 1844. It was absorbed, together with the Birmingham and Gloucester Railway, by the Midland Company in 1845 and this became part of that Company's main line to the West of England.

50. Taff Vale Railway

(See 47 – **Map 1842**)

51. Llanelly Railway

(See 17 – **Map 1836**)

52. Bristol and Exeter Railway

(See 50 – **Map 1842**)

53. London and Southampton (London and South Western) Railway

(*See* 31 – **Map 1839**)

54. London and Greenwich Railway

(*See* 16 – **Map 1836**)

55. The Croydon Railway

(*See* 33 – **Map 1839**)

56. London and Brighton Railway

(*See* 56 – **Map 1842**)

The section of the line from Shoreham to Worthing was opened in November, 1845.

57. South Eastern Railway

(*See* 55 – **Map 1842**)

The Tonbridge to Tunbridge Wells branch was opened in September, 1845, and the 10 miles branch from Paddock Wood to Maidstone was brought into operation in September, 1844. A further portion of their main line form Ashford to a temporary station at Folkestone was opened in June, 1843, and the Company took the opportunity of purchasing the harbour at Folkestone from the Exchequer Commissioners. Arrangements were then made with the Commercial Steam Packet Company to put on a daily service to Boulogne, whereby the journey from London to the French port could be covered in six hours at a cost of 25s., 17s, and 12s. respectively for 1st, 2nd, and 3rd class passengers. The main line extension to Dover from the temporary terminus at Folkestone was opened in February, 1844.

58. Thames and Medway Canal Company (Gravesend and Rochester Railway)

Company formed in 1845.

In 1845 the Company obtained an Act for the construction of a line – 7 miles – between Gravesend and Rochester (Strood) on the southern bank of their then existing canal. Difficulties were presented by the portion of the line where the canal ran through a 2 mile tunnel approaching the Medway at Strood. Through this tunnel the single line was carried on timber supports over part of the canal so as to leave a certain amount of room for navigation. The carriages ran so close to the wall of the tunnel that special wire grills had to be placed over the carriage windows to prevent passengers injuring themselves by putting their heads out. The line was opened in February, 1845, and, with three engines at their disposal, the Company provided a service of six trains per day in each direction. By September of the same year this had been increased to twenty trains a day.

The line was purchased by the South Eastern Railway Company in 1846 and was closed in November of that year in order that the canal through the tunnel could be filled in and a double line of rails substituted for the single track. It was opened again for traffic in August, 1847.

59. Canterbury and Whitstable Railway

(*See* 18 – **Map 1836**)

60. Bodmin and Wadebridge Railway

(*See* 19 – **Map 1836**)

61. Hayle Railway

(*See* 37 – **Map 1839**)

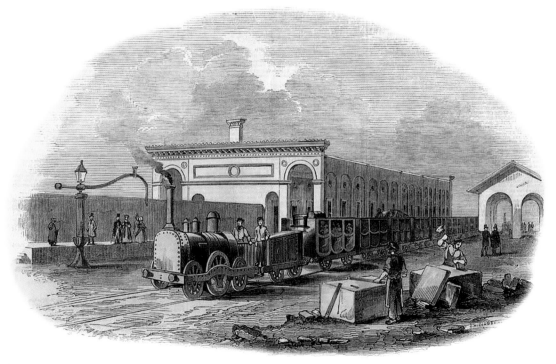

CAMBRIDGE STATION – OPENING OF THE LINE TO CAMBRIDGE AND ELY 1845 – EASTERN COUNTIES RAILWAY

1845

AMALGAMATIONS AND CONSOLIDATIONS

Warrington and Newton Railway – Absorbed by the Grand Junction in 1835

Wigan Branch Railway, Preston and Wigan Railway – Amalgamated under the title of North Union Railway, 1834

Leeds and Selby – Purchased by the York and North Midland, 1844

North Union, Bolton and Preston – Amalgamated retaining the name North Union, 1844.

Sheffield and Rotherham – Absorbed by the Midland, 1844

London and Greenwich – Leased in perpetuity to the South Eastern, 1845

Norwich and Brandon, Yarmouth and Norwich – Amalgamated on equal terms as Norfolk Railway, 1844

Birmingham and Gloucester, Bristol and Gloucester – Amalgamated as Birmingham and Bristol, 1845

Erewash Valley – Purchased by Midland, 1845

Hull and Selby – Leased to York and North Midland, 1845

Great North of England – Leased jointly by Newcastle and Darlington Junction, Midland, and York and North Midland.

Whitby and Pickering – Purchased by the York and North Midland, 1845

Liverpool and Manchester, Bolton and Leigh, Leigh and Kenyon Junction – Absorbed by Grand Junction, 1845

Durham Junction Railway – Purchased by the Newcastle and Darlington Junction Company, 1843

Brandling Junction Railway – Purchased by the Newcastle and Darlington Junction Railway, 1845

Chester and Crewe Railway – Amalgamated with Grand Junction, 1844

Midland Counties, North Midland, Birmingham and Derby Junction – Amalgamated as Midland Railway Company, 1844

Northern and Eastern – Leased in perpetuity to Eastern Counties, January, 1844

Cheltenham and Great Western Union – Absorbed by the Great Western Company, 1843

Oxford Branch – Absorbed by the Great Western, 1844

Clarence Railway, Great North of England – Leased to Hartlepool Dock Railway, 1845

Canterbury and Whitstable – Leased to South Eastern, 1844

Manchester, Bury and Rossendale, Blackburn, Burnley, Accrington and Colne Extension – Amalgamated as East Lancashire, July 1845

West London Company (too small to be shown on the map) – Leased jointly by London and Birmingham, and Great Western, 1845

Guildford Junction – Purchased by London and South Western, 1845

Bricklayers Arms Branch (from London and Croydon) (too small to be shown on map) – Purchased by South Eastern, 1845

Map 1846

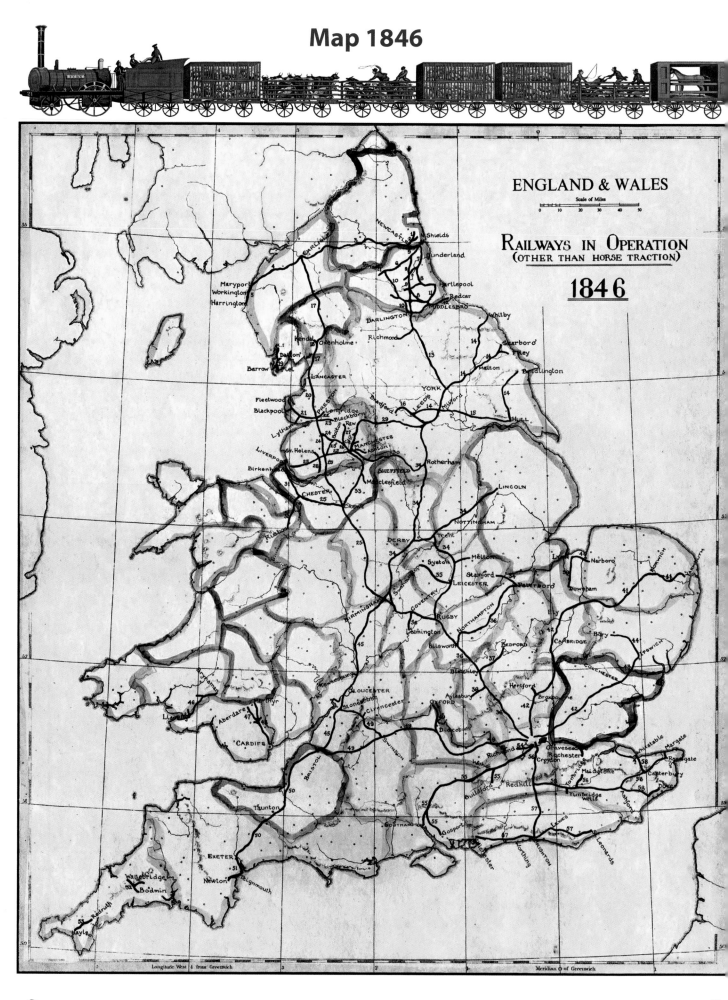

ENGLAND & WALES

Scale of Miles

RAILWAYS IN OPERATION
(OTHER THAN HORSE TRACTION)

1846

RAILWAYS IN OPERATION
1846

This was the ninth year of Queen Victoria's reign. It saw the end of Peel's second ministry (1841 – 1846) and the beginning of Lord John Russell's ministry (1846 – 1852). In June, new free trade proposals having provoked stiff resistance from a group of Conservatives led by Disraeli, the Corn Laws were finally repealed and Peel's ministry was overthrown.

In India peace was made with the Sikhs, the Punjab being brought under British control.

So far as science and discovery are concerned, it was in this year that an American, Elias Howe, patented the first practical sewing machine, gun-cotton was invented by Schonbein and protoplasm was discovered by Mohl.

1. Sedghill to Percy Main

(*See* 1 – **Map 1842**)

2. Newcastle and North Shields Railway (Newcastle and Berwick Railway)

(*See* 2 – **Map 1839**)

3. Newcastle and Carlisle Railway

(*See* 1 – **Map 1836**)

4. Maryport and Carlisle Railway

(*See* 12 – **Map 1842**)

5. Whitehaven Junction Railway

Company formed 1844.
Intended as an extension of 12 miles to the Maryport and Carlisle line from Maryport to Whitehaven via Workington. The 5½ miles from Maryport to Workington was opened in January, 1846, and the remaining section was finally opened to passenger traffic in March, 1847. Arrangements led to the operation of the railway by the Maryport and Carlisle Railway Co., as each section became available.

6. Pontop and South Sheilds Railway

(*See* 4 – **Map 1839**)

7. Durham and Sunderland Railway

(*See* 3 – **Map 1836**)

8. Hartlepool Dock and Railway

(*See* 4 – **Map 1836**: *also Clarence Railway,* 5 – **Map 1836**: *Gt. North of England Railway,* 13 – **Map 1842**: *and Amalgamations and Consolidations listed on page 115 (1845 section)*

9. Newcastle and Darlington Junction Railway

(*See* 10 – **Map 1845**: *also Brandling Junction Railway,* 3 – **Map 1839**: *Durham Junction Railway,* 6 – **Map 1839**: *and Amalgamations and Consolidations listed on page 115 (1845 section)*

10. Stockton and Darlington Railway

(*See* 6 – **Map 1836**)

11. Stockton and Hartlepool Railway

(*See* 10 – **Map 1842**)

12. Middlesborough and Redcar Railway

Company formed in 1845.
A line of 7½ miles to connect the two towns was opened in June, 1846. It was leased by the Stockton and Darlington Railway Company in 1847 and was subsequently merged into the North Eastern Railway Company in 1863 and later formed part of the L.N.E.R. system.

13. Great North of England Railway (York and Newcastle Railway)

(*See* 13 – **Map 1842**)

14. York and North Midland Railway

(*See* 11 – **Map 1839**: *also Whitby and Pickering Railway,* 7 – **Map 1836**: *Leeds and Selby Railway,* 8 – **Map 1836**: *and Amalgamations and Consolidations listed on page 115 (1845 section)*
The extension of 6 miles to Filey and the line from Hull to Bridlington, 31 miles, were both opened in October, 1846.

15. Hull and Selby Railway

(*See* 17 – **Map 1842**)

16. Leeds and Bradford Railway

Company formed in 1843.
A line of 13½ miles, via Shipley and the Aire valley, to connect Leeds and Bradford and a branch line of 1¼ miles from the Wellington Street Station of the Company to join the North Midland line near its terminus in Hunslet were opened in July, 1846. The Company was leased to the Midland Railway the same year, after a lease to the Manchester and Leeds Railway had been repudiated. Hudson was concerned in the negotiations for the Midland lease and was suspected of some duplicity in the matter.

ROYAL HOTEL COACH OFFICE,
Cheltenham,
IMPROVED SAFETY & ELEGANT LIGHT POST COACHES,
DAILY TO THE FOLLOWING PLACES.

LONDON The Magnet Safety Coach, every Morning at ½ past Six o'clock thro' Northleach, Burford, Witney, Oxford, Henley, Maidenhead, Slough & Hounslow.

LONDON Royal Veteran, every Morning at ½ past Eight thro' Northleach, Burford, Witney, Oxford, Wycomb & Uxbridge.

OXFORD & LONDON Two Day Coach, every day except Sundays at Twelve o'clock, Sleeps at Oxford.

OXFORD Coaches, every Morning at ½ past Six & ½ past Eight o'clock.

BATH The Original Post Coach, every day except Sundays at Nine o'clock through Gloucester & Rodborough.

BATH The York House Coach, every day except Sundays at Two o'clock through Painswick & Stroud.

BRISTOL The Traveller, every day except Sundays at Twelve o'clock thro' Gloucester & Newport.

BRISTOL The Royal Pilot, through Gloucester every Monday, Wednesday, & Friday, at ½ past One o'clock.

EXETER The Traveller, every day except Sundays, at Twelve thro' Gloucester, Bristol, Bridgewater, Taunton, Wellington, Collumpton, & Exeter, where it meets Coaches for Plymouth.

GLOUCESTER Accommodation Coaches every Morning at Nine, ½ past Nine & Twelve, o'clock Afternoon at ½ past One, Three Five & Seven o'clock, in the Evening.

TEWKESBURY Coaches every Morning except Sundays, at Eight & Twelve, Afternoon at ½ past One, every Evening at 8.

MALVERN The Mercury, every Morning at ¼ before Eight, except Sundays, to Essingtons Hotel, Malvern Wells, arrives at Eleven o'clock, leaves Malvern at Five.

LIVERPOOL The Magnet, every Tuesday, Thursday & Saturday, at Twelve o'clock, thro' Worcester, Birmingham, Walsall, Stafford, Stone, & Newcastle.

LIVERPOOL The Aurora, every day except Sundays, at ½ past one o'clock sleeping at Birmingham.

MANCHESTER The Traveller, every day except Sundays, at Twelve o'clock, thro' Worcester, Sleeping at Birmingham.

SHEFFIELD The Amity, every day except Sundays, at Twelve o'clock, through Burton, Derby, & Chesterfield.

CHESTER The Dispatch, every day except Sundays, thro' Newport & Fernhill.

BIRMINGHAM The Traveller, thro' Worcester, every day except Sundays, at Twelve o'clock.

BIRMINGHAM The York House Coach, thro' Worcester every day except Sundays, at ½ past One o'clock.

BIRMINGHAM The Mercury, thro' Worcester, every Morning at Eight.

WORCESTER Coaches, every Morning at Eight & Twelve, also at ½ past one o'clock, in the Afternoon.

WOLVERHAMPTON The Everlasting, every Morning at Eight, except Sundays.

COVENTRY The Pilot, thro' Evesham, Alcester, Stratford, Warwick, & Leamington, every day except Sundays, at ½ past one o'clock.

FLY WAGGONS & VANS TO LONDON
on Tuesdays Thursdays & Saturdays at Twelve o'clock & arrives the following Night

THOMAS HAINES Junr & Co ____ PROPRIETORS.

NB. Every possible comfort & accommodation afforded to those who may be pleased to honour this Establishment with their patronage.

COACHES SENT TO ANY PART OF THE TOWN TO TAKE UP IF REQUIRED.

S.Y.Griffith & C° Copper Plate Printers.

118

17. Lancaster and Carlisle Railway

Company formed in 1844.

This project formed part of the scheme for connecting England with Scotland as recommended in a report of the Government Commissioners appointed in 1839 which contemplated a line of 70 miles to join the two towns. Both the Grand Junction and North Union Companies volunteered to give financial assistant to the undertaking. As the line crossed Shep Fells it involved several miles of a gradient of 1 in 75. The first 20 miles from Lancaster to Oxenholme was opened in September, 1846 and the opening of the remaining section of the line over Shap summit to Carlisle (50 miles) was achieved in December of the same year.

18. Kendal and Windermere Railway

Company formed in 1845.

Intended to connect Windermere with the Lancaster and Carlisle Railway at Oxenholme, a distance of 10¼ miles. The first two miles from Oxenholme to Kendal was opened in September, 1846, and the remaining 8¼ miles section to Windermere in April, 1847, The Company was leased perpetuity to the Lancaster and Carlisle Railway Company in 1857 and was subsequently merged into the London and North Western Railway system two years later.

19. Furness Railway

Company formed in 1844.

A local line unconnected with the main railway system, intended chiefly for the purpose of connecting the mines in the Furness district of Lancashire with the port of Barrow. Its lines joined Barrow and Rampside on the one hand with Kirkby Irleth and Dalton on the other, and connected with a steamer service across Morecambe Bay from Fleetwood. The total mileage of 15 miles was opened for goods traffic in July, 1846, and for passenger traffic in December 1846.

20. Lancaster and Preston Railway

(*See* 18 – **Map 1842**)

21. Preston and Wyre Railway

(*See 19 – Map 1843*)
The Lytham branch, 4¾ miles, was opened in February, 1846, and the Blackpool branch, 3¼ miles, was opened in April the same year.

22. Preston and Longridge Railway

(*See 20 – **Map 1842**)

OPENING OF EASTERN UNION RAILWAY JUNE 6TH 1846

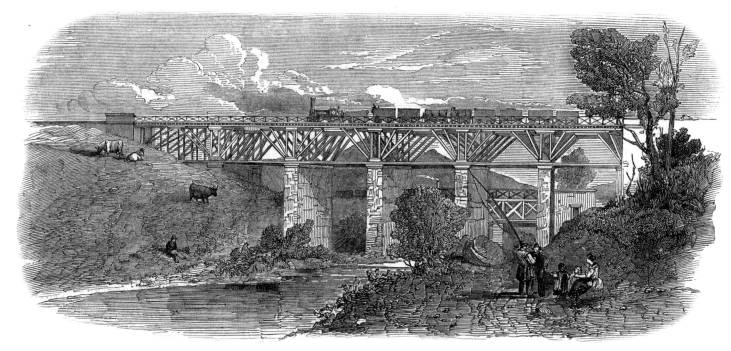

ALDERBOTTOM VIADUCT ON THE EAST LANCASHIRE RAILWAY

23. Blackburn and Preston Railway (East Lancashire Railway)

Company formed in 1844.
The line of 9½ miles formed a junction with the North Union Railway at Farrington to Blackburn and was opened in June, 1846. The Company was absorbed by the East Lancashire Railway later the same year.

24. North Union Railway

(*See Preston and Wigan Railway, 13 –* **Map 1839***; Wigan Branch Railway, 12 –* **Map 1836***; Bolton and Preston Railway, 23 –* **Map 1842***; and Amalgamations and Consolidations listed on page 115 (1845 section).*)

25. Grand Junction Railway (London and North Western Railway)

(*See 23 –* **Map 1839***; also Liverpool and Manchester Railway, 9 –* **Map 1836***; Bolton and Leigh Railway, 13 –* **Map 1836***; Leigh and Kenyon Junction Railway, 14 –* **Map 1836***; Warrington and Newton Railway, 11 –* **Map 1836***; Chester and Crewe Railway, 33 –* **Map 1842***; and Amalgamations and Consolidations listed on page 115 (1845 section).*)

26. Manchester and Bolton Railway

(*See 20 –* **Map 1839**)

27. East Lancashire Railway

Company Formed in 1845. (created by Act of Parliament 1846)
This company was in fact an amalgamation of the Blackburn, Burnley, Accrington and Colne Railway on obtaining its Act and the Manchester, Bury and Rossendale Railway Company under a new title.

A line of 14 miles from Clifton Junction to Rawtenstall was opened in September, 1846, access to Manchester being dependant on the 4 miles of the Manchester, Bolton and Bury Railway from Clifton Junction to Salford. Sanctioned originally as a local line to serve the Rossendale district, by following an energetic policy it soon grew to embrace the towns of Blackburn, Burnley, Accrington and Colne. By amalgamation with the Blackburn and Preston Railway it obtained an exchange point for its traffic at that important junction, and its further amalgamation with the Liverpool, Ormskirk, and Preston gave it access to Liverpool. At Colne it was to join the Colne extension of the Leeds and Bradford, so providing another route from Lancashire into Yorkshire.

28. St. Helens and Runcorn Gap Railway

(*See 10 –* **Map 1836**)

29. Manchester and Leeds Railway

(*See 21 –* **Map 1839**)

An extension of 5 miles to Ashton was opened in April, 1846.

30. Sheffield, Ashton and Manchester Railway

(*See 31 –* **Map 1842**)

31. Chester and Birkenhead Railway

(*See 32 –* **Map 1842**)

32. Shrewsbury and Chester Railway

Company formed in 1845.
This company was first incorporated as the Shrewsbury, Oswestry and Chester Railway which amalgamated with the North Wales Mineral Company in 1846 as the Shrewsbury and Chester Railway. A line of 23½ miles was authorized under the new company from Shrewsbury to a junction at Cefn Mawr.

The first section from Saltney Junction to Ruabon – 15 miles – and Saltney Branch to the River Dee – ¾ mile – were opened in November, 1846. This necessitated bringing into use about 2 miles of the Chester and Holyhead Railway, then under construction, as it had previously been arranged that the N.W.M. Co., were to run their trains over that Company's line from Saltney to Chester rather than incur the expense of another bridge over the River Dee.

The use of this bridge before the Chester and Holyhead Railway Co. were in full operation resulted in disaster. After six months use the cast-iron girders of a span of the Dee Bridge broke under the stress of an evening train from Chester to Ruabon. All the carriages crashed into the river below, killing five passengers and injuring the remainder.

33. Manchester and Birmingham Railway (London and North Western Railway)

(*See* 34 – **Map 1842**)

34. Midland Railway

(*See Sheffield and Rotherham Railway, 22 –* **Map 1839**; *North Midland Railway, 36 –* **Map 1842**; *Birmingham and Derby Junction Railway, 25 –* **Map 1839**; *Midland Counties Railway, 24 –* **Map 1839**; *and Amalgamations and Consolidations listed on page 115 (1845 section).*)

The following sections of lines were opened during 1846. Nottingham to Lincoln – 33 miles – in August; Syston to Melton Mowbray – 10¼ miles – in September, and Stamford to Peterborough – 12¾ miles – in October.

35. Leicester and Swannington Railway (Midland Railway)

(*See* 15 – **Map 1836**)

36. London and Birmingham Railway (London and North Western Railway)

(*See* 27 – **Map 1839**)

37. London and North Western Railway

Company formed in 1846 with the amalgamation of the London and Birmingham, Grand Junction and Manchester and Birmingham Railways. The Bletchley to Bedford branch line of 16¼ miles was opened in November, 1846.

38. Aylesbury Railway (London and Birmingham Railway)

(*See* 28 – **Map 1839**)

39. Lynn and Ely Railway

Company formed in 1845.

A main line of 26 miles was sanctioned from Lynn to a junction with the Eastern Counties Railway at Ely with a Lynn Harbour branch of 1¾ miles and a further branch of 10 miles from Watlington to Wisbech. A section of 10¾ from Lynn to Downham Market and the Harbour branch were both opened in October, 1846.

The Company amalgamated with the Lynn and Dereham Railway and the Lynn and Huntingdon Railway in 1847 under the title of East Anglian Railway Company which was subsequently merged into the Great Eastern Railway in 1862.

MIDLAND RAILWAY

40. Lynn and Dereham Railway

Company formed in 1845.

Intended as a main line of 26¾ miles to connect the two towns. The first section of 8¾ miles from Lynn to Narborough was opened in October, 1846. The Company amalgamated with the Lynn and Ely Railway, see 39 above, and the Ely and Huntingdon Railway under the title of East Anglian Railway in 1847.

41. Norfolk Railway

(*See Yarmouth and Norwich Railway, 45 – **Map 1845**; Norwich and Brandon Railway, 46 – **Map 1845**; and Amalgamations and Consolidations listed on page 115 (1845 section)*)

42. Eastern Counties Railway

(*See 30 – **Map 1839**, 44 & 45 – **Map 1842**, and 47 – **Map 1845***)

43. Eastern Union Railway

Company formed in 1844.

Intended as an extension of 17 miles of the Eastern Counties lines from their terminus at Colchester to Ipswich. The line was opened in June, 1846.

44. Ipswich, Bury and Norwich Railway

Company formed in 1845.

The Company was first incorporated as the Ipswich and Bury Railway with the intention of building a line connecting the two towns but, on obtaining an Act for an extension to Norwich in 1846, the Company forthwith changed its name to the Ipswich, Bury and Norwich Railway. The line connecting Ipswich and Bury – 26¾ miles – was opened for freight traffic in November 1846 and for passenger traffic a month later. It was worked by the Eastern Union Railway Company and was eventually absorbed by them in 1847.

45. Birmingham and Bristol Railway

(*See Birmingham and Gloucester Railway, 41 – **Map 1842**; Bristol and Gloucester Railway, 49 – **Map 1845**; and Amalgamations and Consolidations listed on page 115 (1845 section)*)

46. Llanelly Railway

(*See 17 – **Map 1836***)

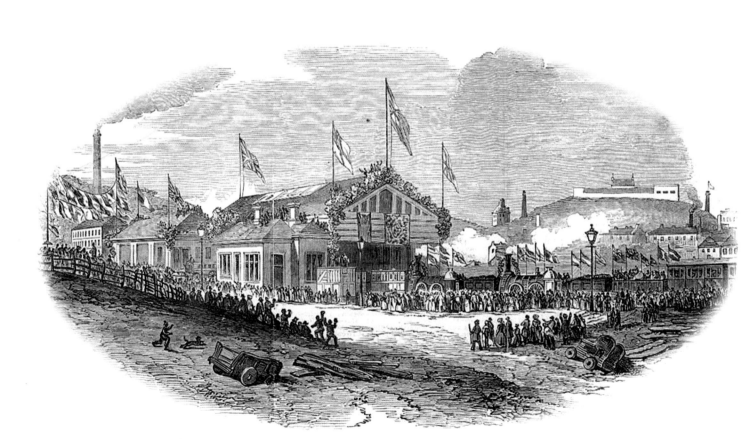

OPENING OF THE SOUTH DEVON RAILWAY AT PLYMOUTH

47. Aberdare Railway

Company formed in 1845.

Intended as a junction with Taff Vale Railway from Navigation House to Aberdare with a branch to Cwmbach Colliery, a total of 9½ miles. It was opened in August, 1846, and leased by the Taff Vale Company in 1847. The Company was subsequently merged into the Gt. Western Railway system.

48. Taff Vale Railway

(*See* 47 – **Map 1842**)

49. Great Western Railway

(*See* 29 – **Map 1839**; 48 – **Map 1842** *and* 48 – **Map 1845**)

50. Bristol and Exeter Railway

(*See* 50 – **Map 1842**)

51. South Devon Railway

Company formed in 1844.

Intended as an extension of the Bristol and Exeter Railway from the latter city to the port of Plymouth.

This main line of 52 miles followed the coast line to Newton Abbott, whence by a series of steep gradients, a terminus at Laira (Plymouth) was reached. The section of line from Exeter to Teignmouth – 15 miles – was opened in May, 1846, and a further 5½ miles to Newton Abbott was opened in December the same year. The line was finally completed to Plymouth and opened in May, 1848. A branch from Aller Junction to Torquay was opened the following December.

52. Bodmin and Wadebridge Railway

(*See* 19 – **Map 1836**)

53. Hayle Railway (West Cornwall Railway)

(*See* 37 – **Map 1839**)

54. Richmond Railway (London and South Western Railway)

Company formed in 1845.

A line of 6 miles intended to connect Richmond with a junction with the London and South Western line at Battersea. It was opened in July, 1846, and purchased by the London and South Western Company a month later.

55. London and Southampton Railway (London and South Western Railway)

(*See* 31 – **Map 1839**)

56. Croydon Railway (London, Brighton and South Coast Railway)

(*See* 33 – **Map 1839**)

57. London and Brighton Railway (London, Brighton and South Coast Railway)

(*See* 56 – **Map 1842**)

The title of the Company was changed in 1846 from "London and Brighton" on amalgamation with the "London and Croydon" Company.

The following extensions were opened in 1846:- Worthing to Littlehampton, 7½ miles, in March; Brighton to Lewes, 8 miles, Littlehampton to Chichester, 10½ miles, and Lewes to Bulverhythe, 24½ miles in June and St. Leonards extension, ½ mile, in November.

58. South Eastern Railway

(*See* 55 – **Map 1842**; 57 – **Map 1845**; *also London and Greenwich Railway,* 16 – **Map 1836**; *Canterbury and Whitstable Railway –* 18 – **Map 1836**; *and Amalgamations and Consolidations listed on page 115 (1845 section)*)

The following sections of lines were opened in 1846:- Ashford to Canterbury, 14½ miles, in February; Canterbury to Ramsgate, 15¾ miles in April; Tunbridge Wells to Mount Pleasant, 1 mile, in November; Ramsgate to Margate, 3¾ miles in December.

59. Gravesend and Rochester Railway (South Eastern Railway)

(*See* 58 – **Map 1845**)

Eastern Counties and Thames Junction Railway (Eastern Counties Railway)

(*Too small to be shown on map*)

Company formed in 1844.

A short line of 2½ miles, promoted under the auspices of the Eastern Counties and Northern and Eastern Railways for the purpose of connecting their lines at Stratford with the River Thames near the mouth of the River Lea. It was opened in April, 1846, and was purchased by the Eastern Counties Railway Company that same year.

LONDON, BRIGHTON AND SOUTH COAST RAILWAY

LONDON AND SOUTH WESTERN RAILWAY

AMALGAMATIONS AND CONSOLIDATIONS, 1846

Hull and Selby Railway – *Leased jointly by York and North Midland and Manchester and Leeds Railway

North Union Railway – Leased jointly by Grand Junction and Manchester and Leeds Railways.

London and Birmingham Railway, Grand Junction Railway, Manchester and Birmingham Railway – Amalgamated as London and North Western Railway.

Leeds and Bradford Railway – Leased by Midland Railway

Newcastle and North Shields Railway – Absorbed by Newcastle and Berwick Railway

London and Brighton Railway, London and Croydon Railway – Amalgamated as London, Brighton and South Coast Railway.

Aylesbury Railway – Purchased by London and Birmingham Railway

Leicester and Swannington Railway – Absorbed by Midland Railway

Blackburn and Preston Railway – Absorbed by East Lancashire Railway

E.C and Thames Junction Railway – Purchased by Eastern Counties Railway

Richmond Railway – Purchased by London and South Western Railway

Gt. North of England Railway – Leased and subsequently purchased by Newcastle and Darlington Junction Railway, becoming York and Newcastle Railway.

Gravesend and Rochester Railway – Purchased by South Eastern Railway

Hayle Railway – Purchased by West Cornwall Railway

*But by agreement the York and North Midland was to work and manage it to the satisfaction of the Manchester and Leeds. The lease was never formally completed

BRIGHTON VIADUCT ON THE HASTINGS BRANCH OF THE LONDON & BRIGHTON RAILWAY

Map 1847

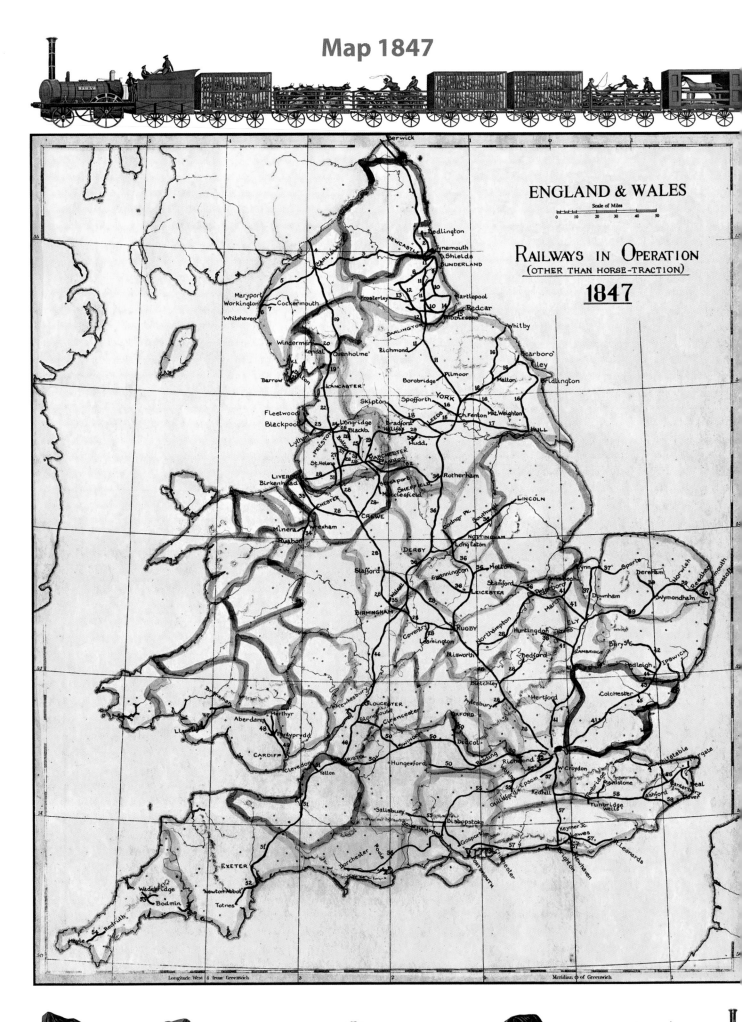

ENGLAND & WALES

Scale of Miles

RAILWAYS IN OPERATION
(OTHER THAN HORSE-TRACTION)

1847

RAILWAYS IN OPERATION
1847

We have now reached the tenth year of Queen Victoria's reign and the second year of Lord John Russell's ministry.

The year 1847 was notable for a series of crimes committed by the Young Irish Party, a radical group which rejected O'Connell's peaceful methods to secure a repeal to the union with England. This led to the suspension of the Habeas Corpus Act for Ireland.

Abroad, the Straits Settlements became a Crown Colony and Liberia was proclaimed independent.

In the world of science and letters, the German philosopher and scientist Helmholtz wrote his thesis "On the Conservation of Energy", the epoch-making paper of the century, and Charlotte Bronte's "Jane Eyre" was published.

1. Newcastle and Berwick Railway
(York, Newcastle and Berwick Railway)

Company formed in 1845.

This project was one of the main ideas of that remarkable man, George Hudson, to have under one control a chain of railways running from Rugby up the eastern side of England to the Scottish Border. The whole scheme of nearly 100 miles comprised not only a main line of 65 miles but also branch along the south of the Tweed and Kelso, and branches to Alnwick and the Bedlington district to serve its ironworks and collieries. A saving was made by utilising the then existing line of the Newcastle and North Shields Railway from Heaton to its terminus at Manors. The Newcastle Corporation were reconciled to the disturbance of property by the prospect of a convenient central station in conjunction with the Newcastle and Carlisle Railway and joined to the Brandling Junction line at Gateshead by a high level bridge. In order to ensure the due subscription of capital, Hudson introduced the Newcastle and Darlington Railway Company to undertake a lease of the line at 5 per cent on the capital spent on its construction.

The opening of the line was accomplished in three sections, the last of which took place in July, 1847, from which date an all rail route between England and Scotland was brought into existence, with the exception of the gaps across the Rivers Tyne and Tweed since the great bridges which had to be constructed over these rivers had not been completed. The Company amalgamated with the York and Newcastle Railway Company the same year under the title of York, Newcastle and Berwick Railway.

2. Blythe and Tyne Railway

This Company incorporated the local line from Seghill to Percy Main (*See* 1 – **Map 1842**). The line was extended to Blythe, 4½ miles in March, 1847, and subsequently a short branch was added to Bedlington Colliery.

3. Newcastle and Carlisle Railway

(*See* 1 – **Map 1836**)

4. Caledonian Railway

Company formed in 1845.

Intended to form a backbone of communication from the Southern border as far as the Forth of Clyde. The section shown on this map from Carlisle was opened in September, 1847, and extended to Beattock, a distance of 39¾ miles.

5. Maryport and Carlisle Railway

(*See* 12 – **Map 1842**)

6. Whitehaven Junction Railway

(*See* 5 – **Map 1846**)

The 4½ mile section of line from Harrington to Whitehaven was opened for Goods traffic in February, 1847, and for Passenger traffic during the following month.

7. Cockermouth and Workington Railway

Company formed in 1845.

A line of 9 miles to connect the two towns was opened in April, 1847. The Company was absorbed by London and North Western Railway in 1866.

8. Pontop and South Shields Railway (Newcastle and Darlington Junction Railway)

(*See* 2 – **Map 1836** *and* 4 – **Map 1839**)

Purchased by the Newcastle and Darlington Railway Company, 1847

9. Durham and Sunderland Railway (Newcastle and Darlington Junction Railway)

(*See* 3 – **Map 1836**)

Company purchased by the Newcastle and Darlington Railway Company, 1847.

10. Hartlepool Dock and Railway

(*See* 4 – **Map 1836**; *also Clarence Railway,* 5 – **Map 1836**; *Great North of England Railway,* 13 – **Map 1842**; *and Amalgamations and Consolidations listed on page 115 (1845 section)*)

CONWAY STATION AND THE GOTHIC ARCH IN THE TOWN HALL

11. Newcastle and Darlington Junction Railway (York and Newcastle Railway)

(*See* 10 – **Map 1845**; *also Brandling Junction Railway, 3 – **Map 1839**; Durham Junction Railway, 6 – **Map 1839**; Great North of England Railway, 13 – **Map 1842**, and Amalgamations and Consolidations listed on page 115 and page 125 (1845 and 1846 section)*)

The branch line of 5¾ miles from Pilmoor to Borobridge was opened in June, 1847. The Company amalgamated with the Newcastle and Berwick Railway as the York, Newcastle and Berwick Railway in 1847.

12. Stockton and Darlington Railway

(*See* 6 – **Map 1836**)

13. Wear Valley Railway

Company formed in 1845.
A line of 10¾ miles from a junction at Wilton-le-Wear to Frosterley was opened in August, 1847, and leased to the Stockton and Darlington Railway Company.

14. Stockton and Hartlepool Railway

(*See* 10 – **Map 1842**)

15. Middlesbrough and Redcar Railway

(*See* 12 – **Map 1846**)

16. York and North Midland Railway

(*See* 11 – **Map 1839**; *also Whitby and Pickering Railway, 7 – **Map 1836**; Leeds and Selby Railway, 8 – **Map 1836**, and Amalgamations and Consolidations listed on page 115 (1845 section)*)

The line from Church Fenton to Spofforth, 13½ miles, was opened in August, 1847; and the lines from York (Bootham Junction) to Market Weighton, 20¾ miles, and from Filey to Bridlington, 13½ miles, were both opened in October, 1847.

17. Hull and Selby Railway

(*See* 17 – **Map 1842**)

18. Leeds and Bradford Railway

(*See* 16 – **Map 1846**)
An extension of 6¼ miles from Shipley to Keighley was opened March, 1847, and a further 9 miles to Skipton was opened the following September.

19. Lancaster and Carlisle Railway

(*See* 17 – **Map 1846**)

20. Kendal and Windemere Railway

(*See* 18 – **Map 1846**)
The 8¼ mile section from Kendal to Windemere was opened in April, 1847.

21. Furness Railway

(*See* 19 – **Map 1846**)

22. Lancaster and Preston Railway

(*See* 18 – **Map 1842**)

23. Preston and Wyre Railway

(*See* 19 – **Map 1842**)

24. Preston and Longridge Railway

(*See* 20 – **Map 1842**)

25. East Lancashire Railway

(*See* 27 – **Map 1846**; *Blackburn and Preston Railway, 23 – **Map 1846**; and Amalgamations and Consolidations listed on page 125 (1846 section)*)

1847 BROAD GAUGE *IRON DUKE* G.W.R.

LONDON AND NORTH WESTERN RAILWAY

26. Bolton, Blackburn, Clitheroe and West Yorkshire Railway

Company formed in 1847.

The Company was formed with the amalgamation of the Blackburn, Darwen and Bolton Railway, incorporated 1845, with the Blackburn, Clitheroe and North Western Junction Railway, incorporated 1846, under a new title. The first section of this Company's line from Blackburn to Sough, 5 miles, was opened in August, 1847. A further section from Sough to Bolton, 8¾ miles, was opened in June, 1848. The Company was subsequently merged into the Lancashire and Yorkshire Railway Company in 1858.

27. North Union Railway

(*See Preston and Wigan Railway, 13 –* **Map 1839**; *Wigan Branch Railway, 12 –* **Map 1836**; *Bolton and Preston Railway, 23 –* **Map 1842**, *and Amalgamations and Consolidations listed on page 115 (1845 section*)

28. London and North Western Railway

(*See 37 –* **Map 1846**; *and Grand Junction Railway, 23 –* **Map 1839**, *also 25 –* **Map 1846**); *Manchester and Birmingham Railway, 34 –* **Map 1842**; *London and Birmingham, 27 –* **Map 1839**; *Aylesbury Railway, 28 –* **Map 1839**, *and Amalgamations and Consolidations listed on page 125 (1846 section*)

A section of line of 49¾ miles from Rugby to Stafford (Trent Valley) was opened in December, 1847.

29. Manchester and Leeds Railway (Lancashire and Yorkshire Railway)

(*See 21 –* **Map 1839** *and Manchester and Bolton Railway, 20 –* **Map 1839** *, and Amalgamations and Consolidations listed in this section*)

The title of the Company was changed to the Lancashire and Yorkshire Railway in 1847.

30. Huddersfield and Manchester Railway

Company formed in 1844.

Authorisation was given in 1845 for a line of 21½ miles from Stalybridge to a junction with the Manchester and Leeds Railway at Heaton Lodge with a Delph branch of 1½ miles. The following year the Company obtained a short branch, 1¼ miles, to Cooper Bridge whereby direct access was available between Huddersfield and Halifax. The first section of the line 3¾ miles from Huddersfield to Heaton Lodge Junction was opened in August, 1847. The Company was absorbed by the London and North Western Railway in 1849.

31. St. Helens and Runcorn Gap Railway

(*See 10 –* **Map 1836**)

32. Sheffield, Ashton and Manchester Railway (Manchester, Sheffield and Lincolnshire Railway)

(*See 31 –* **Map 1842**, *and Amalgamations and Consolidations listed on page 115*)

33. Chester and Birkenhead Railway

(*See 32 –* **Map 1842**)

34. Shrewsbury and Chester Railway

(*See 32 –* **Map 1846**)
A branch line of 6¼ miles from Wrexham to Minera was opened in July, 1847.

35. South Staffordshire Railway

Company formed in 1846.
An Act was first obtained for a line of 9 miles from Dudley to a junction with the Trent Valley, Midlands and Grand Junction Railway at Rushall, with short branches to Darlaston, Bescot, Wyrley and Daw End. The Company absorbed the T.V.M and G.J. in 1846. A further Act was sanctioned in 1847 for a line of 7¼ miles from Walsall to Cannock. The first section of line from Bescot to Walsall, 1½ miles, was opened in November, 1847, and a line of 17¼ miles from Walsall to Wichnor Junction was subsequently opened in April, 1849. Leased to the London and North Western Railway Company in 1861.

36. Midland Railway

(*See Sheffield and Rotherham Railway, 22 –* **Map 1839**; *North Midland Railway, 36 –* **Map 1842**; *Birmingham and Derby Junction Railway, 25 –* **Map 1839**; *Midland Counties Railway, 24 –* **Map 1839**; *Leicester and Swannington Railway, 15 –* **Map 1836**, *and Amalgamations and Consolidations listed on pages 115 and 125 (sections 1845 and 1846).*
A line of 2½ miles from Southwell to Rolleston was opened in July, 1847, and a line from Long Eaton Junction to Codnor Park, 13 miles, was opened the following September.

37. East Anglian Railway

(*See Lynn and Ely Railway, 39 –* **Map 1846**; *Lynn and Dereham Railway, 40 –* **Map 1846**; *Ely and Huntingdon Railway, 38 –* **Map 1847**; *and page 135 Amalgamations and Consolidations (section 1847)*
The following section of lines were opened during 1847, Narborough to Swaffham – 5¾ miles, and St. Ives to Huntingdon, 5¼ miles were both opened in August. Downham to Ely, 14¼ miles, and Swaffham to Sporle, 3 miles, were opened in October.

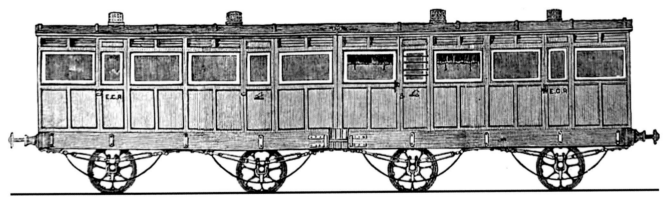

SIDE VIEW OF IMPROVED RAILWAY CARRIAGE

INTERIOR OF COMPARTMENT OF FIRST CLASS CARRIAGE

INTERIOR OF COMPARTMENT OF SECOND CLASS CARRIAGE

38. Ely and Huntingdon Railway
(East Anglian Railway)

Company formed in 1845.
An Act was originally obtained for a line of 22 miles to join the two towns. A small section of 5¼ miles from St. Ives to Huntingdon was opened in August, 1847. (See 37 above.) This was worked by the Eastern Counties Railway in conjunction with their Cambridge to St. Ives Branch which opened on the same day. The Company became one of the constituent parts of the East Anglian Railway in 1847.

39. Norfolk Railway

(*See Yarmouth and Norwich Railway, 45 –* **Map 1845**; *Norwich and Brandon Railway, 46 –* **Map 1845**; *and Amalgamations and Consolidations listed on page 115 (section 1845).*)
The branch line from Wymondham to Dereham was opened in February, 1847.

40. Lowestoft Railway and Harbour Branch

Company formed in 1845.
Intended as a line of 11¼ miles from Lowestoft to connect with the Yarmouth and Norwich (East Anglian) line at Reedham and a short harbour branch. The line was opened for Goods traffic in May, 1847, and or Passenger traffic the following July.

41. Eastern Counties Railway

(*See 30 –* **Map 1839**; *44 & 45 –* **Map 1842**; *and 47 –* **Map 1845**)
The following lines were opened during 1847. Ely to Peterborough, 28¼ miles, in January; March to Wisbech, 7¾ miles, in May; Thames Wharf to North Woolwich, 2½ miles, and a curve at Stratford Junction, ¼ mile, in June, and Cambridge (Chesterton Junction) to St. Ives, 13¼ in August.

42. Ipswich, Bury and Norwich Railway
(Eastern Union)

(*See 44 –* **Map 1846**, *and Amalgamations and Consolidations on page 125 (section 1846)*)

43. Eastern Union Railway

(*See 43 –* **Map 1846**, *and page 125 Amalgamations and Consolidations (section 1846)*)

44. Eastern Union and Hadleigh Junction Railway
(Eastern Union)

Company formed in 1846.
Act originally obtained for a line from Bentley to Hadleigh, 6½ miles, with a curve at Bentley South of ¼ miles. The line was opened in August, 1847, and was purchased by the Eastern Union Railway the same year.

45. Colchester, Stour Valley, Sudbury and
Halstead Railway

Company formed in 1846.
An Act was originally obtained for lines from Marks Tey to Sudbury, 12 miles; Chappel to Halstead, 5¾ miles; and an extension to Hythe of 1½ miles. A peculiarity of the Act was that the Lords Committee insisted on the insertion of a clause making it obligatory on the Company's part to provide a cottage at every level crossing. The 1½ mile extension from Colchester to Hythe was opened in April 1847, for Goods traffic only. The Marks Tey to Sudbury branch was subsequently opened in July, 1849, in which year the Company was leased to the Eastern Union Railway.

46. Birmingham and Bristol Railway

(*See Birmingham and Gloucester, 41 –* **Map 1842**; *Bristol and Gloucester Railway, 49 –* **Map 1845**; *and Amalgamations and Consolidations listed on page 115 (section 1845)*)

47. Llanelly Railway

(*See 17 –* **Map 1836**)

48. Aberdare Railway

(*See 47 –* **Map 1846**)

49. Taff Vale Railway

(*See 47 –* **Map 1842**)

50. Great Western Railway

(*See 29 –* **Map 1839**; *48 –* **Map 1842**, *and 48 –* **Map 1845**)
The line from Reading to Hungerford, 25½ miles, was opened in December, 1847.

51. Bristol and Exeter Railway

(*See 50 –* **Map 1842**)
The branch line from Yatton to Clevedon was opened in July, 1847.

52. South Devon Railway

(*See 51 –* **Map 1846**)
The extension from Newton Abbot to Totnes, 8¾ miles, was opened in July, 1847.

53. Bodmin and Wadebridge Railway

(*See 19 –* **Map 1836**)

54. West Cornwall Railway

(*See Hayle Railway, 37 –* **Map 1839**, *and Amalgamations and Consolidations listed on page 115 (section 1845)*)

55. London and South Western Railway

(*See London and Southampton Railway, 31 – **Map 1839**; Richmond Railway, 54 – **Map 1846**, and Amalgamations and Consolidations listed on page 125 (section 1846)*)
The line from Bishopstoke to Salisbury, 22 miles, was opened in March, 1847.

56. Southampton and Dorchester Railway

Company formed in 1845.
A main line of 60 miles with a 2-mile branch line to Poole was authorized. The line followed a circuitous course via Brockenhurst, Ringwood, Wimborne and Wareham in order to afford the maximum accommodation to the inhabitants of a somewhat sparsely populated region. The promoters of the Company succeeded in inducing the London and South Western Railway Company to rent the line when constructed for £20,000 per annum, and a half share of any surplus profits. The completed line was opened throughout in June, 1847 and was worked by the London and South Western pending an arrangement for amalgamation which came into effect in 1848.

57. London, Brighton and South Coast Railway

(*See London and Brighton Railway, 56 – **Map 1842**; Croydon Railway, 33 – **Map 1839**, and Amalgamations and Consolidations listed on page 125 (section 1846)*)
The following extensions were opened during 1847; Chichester to Havant, 8¾ miles, in March; West Croydon to Epsom, 8 miles, in May; Havant to Portsmouth, 7¼ miles, in June; Keymer Junction to Lewes, 9 miles, in October and from Lewes to Newhaven, 5¾ miles, in December.

58. South Eastern Railway

(*See 55 – **Map 1842**; 57 – **Map 1845**; also London and Greenwich Railway, 16 – **Map 1836**; Canterbury and Whitstable Railway, 18 – **Map 1836**; Gravesend and Rochester Railway, 58 – **Map 1845**; and Amalgamations and Consolidations listed on pages 115 and 125 (sections 1845 and 1846)*)
The branch line form Minster to Deal, 8¾ miles, was opened in July, 1847.

NINE ELMS RAILWAY STATION – LONDON TERMINUS OF THE LONDON AND SOUTH WESTERN RAILWAY

WEEDON VIADUCT ON THE LONDON TO BIRMINGHAM RAILWAY 1839

AMALGAMATIONS AND CONSOLIDATIONS, 1847

Manchester and Bolton Railway – Absorbed by Manchester and Leeds (1846)

Aberdare Railway – Leased by Taff Vale Railway

Eastern Union and Hadleigh Junction Railway – Purchased by Eastern Union.

Ely and Huntingdon Railway/Lynn and Ely Railway/Lynn and Dereham Railway – Amalgamated as East Anglain Railway

Sheffield, Ashton and Manchester Railway/Sheffield and Lincolnshire Railway/Great Grimsby and Sheffield Junction Railway – Amalgamated as Manchester, Sheffield and Lincolnshire Railway

Ipswich, Bury and Norwich Railway – Absorbed by Eastern Union

Lowestoft Railway – Leased by Norfolk Railway

Middlesbrough and Redcar Railway – Leased by Stockton and Darlington Railway

Newcastle and Berwick Railway/York and Newcastle Railway – Amalgamated as York, Newcastle and Berwick Railway

Wear Valley Railway – Leased to Stockton and Darlington Railway

Southampton and Dorchester Railway – Leased to London and South Western Railway

Pontop and South Shields Railway – Purchased by Newcastle and Darlington Junction Railway

Durham and Sunderland Railway – Purchased by Newcastle and Darlington Railway

Manchester and Leeds Railway – Title changed to Lancashire and Yorkshire Railway

Leeds, Dewsbury and Manchester Railway – Absorbed by London and North Western Railway

JENNY LIND STEAM LOCOMOTIVE BUILT FOR THE LONDON AND BRIGHTON RAILWAY

Map 1848

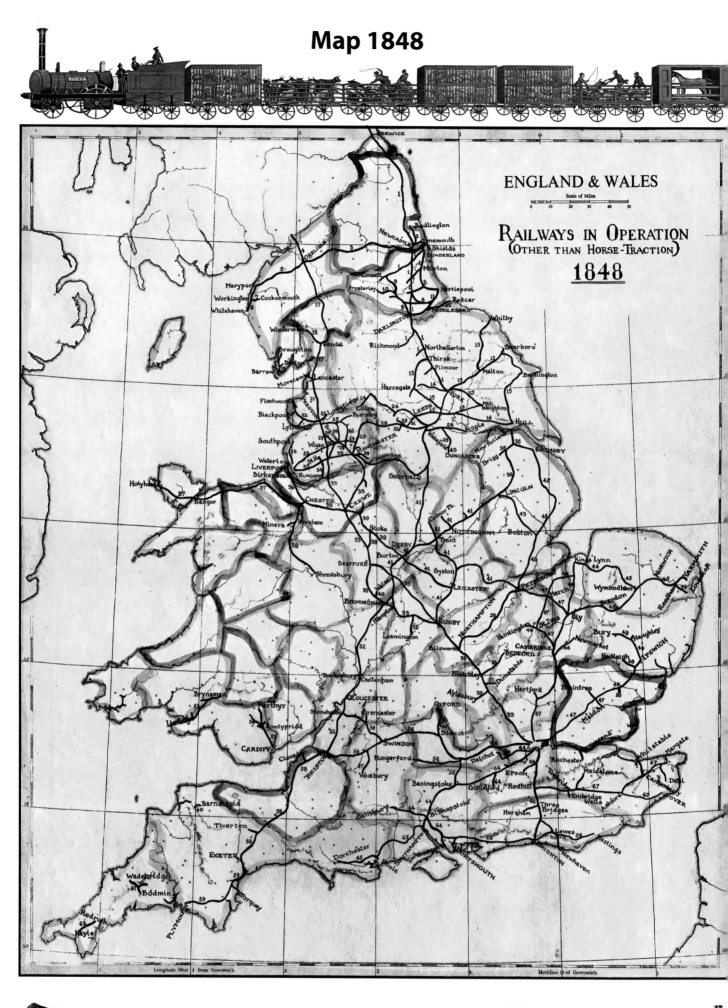

ENGLAND & WALES

Scale of Miles

RAILWAYS IN OPERATION
(OTHER THAN HORSE-TRACTION)
1848

RAILWAYS IN OPERATION
1848

The year 1848 was a year of revolutions. In France, following demonstrations in Paris, King Louis Phillippe abdicated and the Second Republic was proclaimed. This triggered off revolutions in Vienna, Parma and Milan. The Young Ireland Party, who sought repeal of the Irish Union, took advantage of unrest due to famine and the European atmosphere of revolt to stage an insurrection in Tipperary. But it proved abortive. Significantly enough, Marx and Engels issued their famous Communist Manifesto in this year.

At home, a ten-hour working day was established for women and youths, and a Public Health Act, the first sanitary measure on the Statue Book, was passed. J.J. Mills published his Principles of Political Economy.

In the field of letters, Thackeray's Vanity Fair and The Book of Snobs made their appearance and Balzac's Comedie Humaine comprising a hundred volumes was published.

This year brings our history of railways in maps to a close and sadly the year in which the Railway World lost it's famous Father George Stephenson.

The short period between 1836 and 1848 giving rise to the establishment of an extensive railway network covering England and Wales.

1. York, Newcastle and Berwick Railway

(See 1 – **Map 1847** and Newcastle and Darlington Junction Railway, 11 – **Map 1847**; also Pontop and South Shields Railway, 2 – **Map 1836** and 4 – **Map 1839**; Durham and Sunderland Railway, 3 – **Map 1836**; and Amalgamations and Consolidations listed on pages 115, 125 and 135 (sections 1845, 1846 and 1847)

2. Blythe and Tyne Railway

(See 2 – **Map 1847**)

3. Newcastle and Carlisle Railway

(See 1 – **Map 1836**)

4. Caledonian Railway

(See 4 – **Map 1847**)

5. Maryport and Carlisle Railway

(See 12 – **Map 1842**)

6. Whitehaven Junction Railway

(See 5 – **Map 1846**)

7. Cockermouth and Workington Railway

(See 7 – **Map 1847**)

8. Hartlepool Dock Railway

(See 4 – **Map 1836**; also Clarence Railway, 5 – **Map 1836**; Gt. North of England Railway, 13 – **Map 1842**; and Amalgamations and Consolidations listed on page 115 (1845 section)

9. Stockton and Darlington Railway

(See 6 – **Map 1836**)

10. Wear Valley Railway

(See 13 – **Map 1847**)

11. Stockton and Hartlepool Railway

(See 10 – **Map 1842**)

12. Middlesbrough and Redcar Railway

(See 12 – **Map 1846**)

13. Leeds and Thirsk Railway

Company formed in 1845.

This project was fathered in the main by the citizens of Leeds who wanted a more direct access to the North, The scheme materialized and proposals originally comprised a main line of 39½ miles between the two points with branches to Harrogate and Knaresborough. In 1846 further authorization was obtained for a line of 20½ miles from Northallerton to join the Stockton and Hartlepool Company's line at Billingham, and for short junctions with the Stockton and Darlington Railway and Clarence Railway.

The first section of 10½ miles from Ripon to Thirsk Town and junction was opened for goods traffic in January, 1848, and for passenger traffic the following May. Further sections were opened in September, 1848, from Weeton to Wormald Green, 12¾ miles, and From Wormald Green to Ripon, 5 miles. The section of line from Weeton to Leeds, 11¼ miles, was opened in July 1849, and involved the construction of the Bramhope Tunnel, 3763 yards, third in length of those existing at that period.

The northern portion of the Company's line towards Hartlepool was not completed until May, 1852, but accounted for the change of name of the Company to that of Leeds Northern in 1851. In 1854 the Company amalgamated with the York, Newcastle and Berwick and the York and North Midland Railways under the title of North Eastern Railway Company.

14. East and West Yorkshire Junction Railway

Company formed in 1846.

Intended as a line of 15¼ miles from a junction at Poppleton Junction near York to Knaresborough. The first section of line of 14½ miles from Poppleton Junction to Hay Park Lane was opened in October, 1848. A further mile of line from Hay Park Lane to Starbeck, which gave access to Knaresborough by means of a further 1¾ miles, over the Leeds and Thirsk (Leeds Northern) line was opened in 1851.

The Company was absorbed by the York and North Midland Railway in 1851.

15. York and North Midland Railway

(*See* 11 – **Map 1839**; *and* 16 – **Map 1847**; *also Whitby and Pickering Railway*, 7 – **Map 1836**; *Leeds and Selby Railway*, 8 – **Map 1836**; *and Amalgamations and Consolidations listed on page 115 (section 1845)*

The 4¾ miles from Spofforth to Harrogate was opened in July, 1848; from Cliffe Junction (Selby) to Market Weighton – 16¼ miles – in August, 1848.

16. Hull and Selby Railway

(*See* 17 – **Map 1842**)

17. Lancaster and Carlisle Railway

(*See* 17 – **Map 1846**)

18. Kendal and Windermere Railway

(*See* 18 – **Map 1846**)

19. Furness Railway

(*See* 19 – **Map 1846**)

An extension of 3 miles from Kirby to Broughton was opened in February, 1848

20. North Western Railway

Company formed in 1846.

A proposed main line of 42¾ miles forming an extension of the Leeds and Bradford Railway from Skipton to Clapham, where it split, one line running to a junction with the Lancaster and Carlisle Railway, near Tebay, the other, a line of 18¼ miles, proceeding to Lancaster. The Company purchased the Morecambe Harbour and Railway in the year they obtained their Act and in June, 1848, the line of 3½ miles from Lancaster to Morcambe was opened. A section of 25 miles from Skipton to Ingleton was opened in July, 1849, and a 10½ miles section from Lancaster to Wennington in November of the same year. Further openings took place during 1850. The Company was leased in perpetuity to the Midland Railway Company in 1859.

21. Lancaster and Preston Railway

(*See* 18 – **Map 1842**)

22. Preston and Wyre Railway

(*See* 19 – **Map 1842**)

23. Preston and Longridge Railway

(*See* 20 – **Map 1842**)

ACCRINGTON VIADUCT ON THE EAST LANCASHIRE RAILWAY

OGDEN VIADUCT ON THE EAST LANCASHIRE RAILWAY

24. Leeds and Bradford Railway

(*See* 16 – **Map 1846** *and* 18 – **Map 1847**)
The 11¼ miles extension from Skipton to Colne was opened in October, 1848.

25. East Lancashire Railway

(*See* 27 – **Map 1846**; *Blackburn and Preston Railway,* 23 – **Map 1846**); *and Amalgamations and Consolidations listed on page 125 (1846 section)*
The following sections and branch lines were opened during 1848. Rawtenstall to Newchurch – 2 miles, in March; Blackburn to Accrington, 5¼ miles, in June; Accrington to Stubbins, 8 miles, in August, and Accrington to Burnley, 5¼ miles in September.

26. Bolton, Blackburn, Clitheroe and West Yorkshire Railway

(*See* 26 – **Map 1847**)

27. North Union Railway

(*See Preston and Wigan Railway,* 13 – **Map 1839**; *Wigan Branch Railway,* 12 – **Map 1836**; *Bolton and Preston Railway,* 23 – **Map 1842**, *and Amalgamations and Consolidations listed on page 115 (section 1845)*

28. Liverpool, Crosby and Southport Railway

Company formed in 1847.
Intended as a line of 16½ miles from Bootle to Southport. The first section of 13¼ miles from Waterloo to Southport was opened in July, 1848 and the remainder comprising of 3¾ miles from Waterloo to Sandhills Junction was opened in September, 1850. The line was worked by the Lancashire and Yorkshire Railway Company and was eventually purchased by them in 1855.

29. Lancashire and Yorkshire Railway

(*See Manchester and Leeds Railway,* 21 – **Map 1839**; *Manchester and Bolton Railway,* 20 – **Map 1839**; *and Amalgamations and Consolidations listed on page 135 (section 1847)*
The following extensions were opened during 1848; Wakefield to Goole, 27½ miles, in April; Heywood to Bury, and Blue Pitts curve, 4½ miles, in May; Knottingley to Shaftholme Junction, 10¼ miles, in June; Liverpool (Gt. Howard Street) to Wigan, 18½ miles; Hindley to Lostock Junction, 3¾ miles, and Bolton to Bury, 5½ miles in November, and Miles Platting to Manchester (Ardwick), 2 miles, in December.

30. Manchester and Southport Railway

Company formed in 1847.
Intended as a main line of 31¾ miles from Pendleton to Southport with numerous short branches totaling a further 13¼ miles. The Lancashire and Yorkshire Railway Company subscribed more than half the capital with the intention of taking over the Company on obtaining its Act. The first section of the line from Wigan to Hindley, 3 miles, was opened in November, 1848. The Company was eventually absorbed by the Lancashire and Yorkshire Railway in 1855.

31. Leeds, Dewsbury and Manchester Railway (London and North Western Railway)

Company formed in 1845.
Intended as a line of 16¼ miles from Leeds to a junction with the Manchester and Leeds Railway (Lancashire and Yorkshire Railway) at Thornhill with short branches to Birstall and Mirfield. The first section of the line from Thornhill Junction to Leeds (Central), 10½ miles, was formally opened in July, 1848, and opened for public traffic the following September.

The Company was absorbed by the London and North Western Railway in 1847.

Peterborough, 75¾ miles, was 1 hour 50 minutes, with stops at Hitchin and Huntingdon, giving an average speed of 41.3 m.p.h.

44. East Anglain Railway

(See Lynn and Ely Railway, 39 – **Map 1846***; Lynn and Dereham Railway, 40 –* **Map 1846***; Ely and Huntingdon Railway, 38 –* **Map 1847***; and Amalgamations and Consolidations listed on page 135 (section 1847)*

The section from Watlington Junction to Wisbech, 9½ miles, was opened in February, 1848, and from Sporle to Dereham, 9 miles, the following September.

45. Norfolk Railway

(See Yarmouth and Norwich Railway, 45 – **Map 1845***); Norwich and Brandon railway, 46 –* **Map 1845***, and Amalgamations and Consolidations listed on page 115 (1845 section)*

46. Lowestoft Railway and Harbour Branch

(See 40 – **Map 1847***)*

47. Eastern Counties Railway

(See 30 – **Map 1839***; 44 & 45 –* **Map 1842***; 47 –* **Map 1845***, and 41 –* **Map 1847***)*

The following lines were opened during 1848:- St. Ives to March, 19 miles, in March, and from Maldon to Braintree, 12 miles, in October.

48. Newmarket and Chesterford Railway

Company formed in 1846.

Intended as a main line of 16¾ miles with a branch line of 6½ miles from Six Mile Bottom to Cambridge. In 1847 further authorisation was obtained for a line of 28½ miles from Newmarket to Bury, with a branch to Ely and a line of 19¾ miles from Newmarket to Thetford. The main line from Chesterford to Newmarket, 16¾ miles, was opened in April, 1848, and a working arrangement was made with the Eastern Counties railway. Declining receipts and unfavourable working ultimately caused the line to be closed for traffic entirely on 30th June, 1850. It was re-opened again in September the same year, with stock hired from the Eastern Counties Railway and this Company were induced to make a fairer working agreement and a contractor was found to complete the Cambridge branch line. This was opened in October, 1851, and from then the main line existing from Six Mile Bottom to Chesterford was rendered superfluous and closed. The Company was purchased by the Eastern Counties Railways in 1852.

49. Eastern Union Railway

(See 43 – **Map 1846***; also Ipswich, Bury and Norwich Railway, 44 –* **Map 1846***; Eastern Union and Hadleigh Junction Railway, 44 –* **Map 1847***, and Amalgamations and Consolidations listed on page 135 (section 1847)*

The Haughley to Finningham branch, 3¾ miles, was opened in June, 1848.

THE CONWAY TUBULAR BRIDGE ON THE CHESTER & HOLYHEAD RAILWAY

PREPARATIONS FOR RAISING THE SECOND TUBE – BUILDING THE CONWAY TUBULAR BRIDGE
– BUILT BY GEORGE STEPHENSON – OPENED MARCH 1850

TERMINUS OF THE BRIGHTON, DOVER AND CROYDON RAILWAYS AT LONDON BRIDGE

50. Colchester, Stour Valley, Sudbury and Halstead Railway

(*See* 45 – **Map 1847**)

51. Dunstable and London and Birmingham Railway (London and North Western Railway)

Company formed in 1845.
Authorisation was granted for a line of 7 miles from Dunstable to a junction with the London and Birmingham Railway *(See* 27 – **Map 1839**) at Leighton Buzzard on the understanding that the line would be taken over by the London and Birmingham Railway on the Act being obtained. The Company was subsequently merged into the London and North Western Railway in 1846 *(See Amalgamations and Consolidations listed on page 125 (section 1846)* The branch line was opened in May, 1848.

52. Birmingham and Bristol Railway

*(See Birmingham and Gloucester Railway, 41 – **Map 1842**; Bristol and Gloucester Railway, 49 – **Map 1845**; and Amalgamations and Consolidations listed on page 115 (section 1845)*

53. Llanelly Railway

(See 17 – **Map 1836**)

54. Aberdare Railway

(See 47 – **Map 1846**)

55. Taff Vale Railway

(See 47 – **Map 1842**)
The 1¼ mile Bute Docks East branch (Cardiff) was opened during 1848.

56. Great Western Railway

(See 29 – **Map 1839**; 48 – **Map 1842** *and* 48 – **Map 1845**)
The line from Southcote Junction to Basingstoke, 13½ miles, was opened in November, 1848.

57. Wiltshire, Somerset and Weymouth Railway

Company formed in 1845.
This was subsidiary company of the Great Western Railway and was intended to form a main line of 38 miles from Chippenham to Sailsbury where it would join the London and South Western Railway and so form a communication between Southampton and Portsmouth with the West of England. It grew during its period of promotion into a scheme of formidable dimensions by the additional authorisation of extensions to Dorchester and Weymouth with branches to Devizes, Radstock, Sherborne and Bridport. The first section of line to be opened was between Thingley Junction and Westbury, 13¾ miles, in September, 1848. The Company experienced difficulty in raising sufficient money to complete the line sanctioned and it was finally absorbed by the Great Western in 1850 to save it from collapse.

58. Bristol and Exeter Railway

(See 50 – **Map 1842**)
The line from Tiverton Junction to Tiverton, 4¾ miles, was opened in June, 1848.

59. South Devon Railway

(See 51 – **Map 1846**)
The extension from Totnes to Laira (Plymouth), 21¼ miles, was opened in May, 1848, and the branch line from Aller Junction to Torquay, 4 miles, was opened the following December.

60. Taw Vale Railway

Company formed in 1838.
Intended as a small local line of 2¾ miles from Barnstaple to a dock lower down the river at Fremington. The line was not completed until August, 1848, when it was opened for goods traffic only. The Company was subsequently absorbed by the North Devon Railway Company.

61. Bodmin and Wadebridge Railway

(*See* 19 – **Map 1836**)

62. West Cornwall Railway

(*See Hayle Railway, 37 – **Map 1839**, and Amalgamations and Consolidations listed on page 125 (section 1846*)

63. Windsor, Staines and South Western Railway

Company formed in 1847.
Authorisation was granted for the following proposed lines:- Richmond to Windsor (Datchet), 15 miles; Brentford Loop, 7¼ miles; Staines to Pirbright, 13 miles, and a Chertsey branch of 2½ miles. The first section to be completed was from Richmond to Datchet, 14 miles, which was opened in August, 1848. In the same year the Company was leased to the London and South Western Railway and was subsequently merged into that Company in 1850.

64. London and South Western Railway

(*See London and Southampton railway, 31 – **Map 1839**; Richmond Railway, 54 – **Map 1846**, and Amalgamations and Consolidations listed on Page 125 (section 1846*)
The following sections of line were opened during 1848:- Weybridge to Chertsey, 3 miles, in February; Nine Elms to Waterloo, 1¾ miles, in July; and Fareham to Cosham, 5¾ miles, in October.

65. Southampton and Dorchester Railway

(*See* 56 – **Map 1847**)

66. London, Brighton and South Coast Railway

(*See London and Brighton Railway, 56 – **Map 1842**; Croydon Railway, 33 – **Map 1839**, and Amalgamations and Consolidations listed on Page 125 (section 1846*)
The Horsham to Three Bridges branch, 8½ miles, was opened in February, 1848, and the Farlington and Portcreek Junctions to Cosham, 1½ miles, in the following July.

67. South Eastern Railway

(*See 55 – **Map 1842**; 57 – **Map 1845**; also London and Greenwich Railway, 16 – **Map 1836**; Canterbury and Whitstable Railway, 18 – **Map 1836**; Gravesend and Rochester Railway, 58 – **Map 1845**, and Amalgamations and Consolidations listed on pages 115 and 125 (section 1845 and 1846*).

SOUTH EASTERN RAILWAY STATION

1848

AMALGAMATIONS AND CONSOLIDATIONS, 1848

East Lincolnshire Railway – Leased in perpetuity to Great Northern Railway
Windsor, Staines and South Western Railway – Leased to London and South Western Railway

EXPRESS PASSENGER LOCOMOTIVE "ACHERON" – GREAT WESTERN RAILWAY 1848

MAIL COACHES PASS IN THE DARK OF NIGHT – NO MORE CAN THEY MATCH THE SPEED OF THE RAILWAY EXPRESS

PICTURE CREDITS

Railway Maps and Town Plans

Mapseeker Archive Publishing Ltd
www.mapseeker.co.uk
www.oldmapsandimages.co.uk

Special Thanks to Birmingham Archives Services and Heritage
For the sourcing of the original 1805 Town Plan originally drawn by Sherriff,
art worked for this publication.

Pictorial Images, Views, Vistas and other Artefacts.

Mapseeker Archive Publishing Ltd

With special thanks to the following in the sourcing of antique original
resources art worked for this atlas publication

Berian Williams Antique Maps and prints
www.antique-prints-maps.co.uk

Steve Bartrick Maps and prints
www.antiqueprints.com

Ash Rare Books
www.ashrare.com

Marlborough Rare books
www.marlboroughbooks.com

Jonathon Potter Antique Maps Ltd
www.jpmaps.co.uk

Arthur Hook Old Maps and Books
www.hooksbooks.co.uk

Lynn Hughes Artist – Mapseeker Studio
Pencil and charcoal drawing of stagecoaches passing in the night

All of the Early Town Plans featured in this atlas are available as
photographic prints and in a range of other products on
www.mapseeker.co.uk and www.oldmapsandimages.co.uk

DEDICATION TO GEORGE STEPHENSON

George Stephenson was a pioneer of civil and mechanical engineering, a man steadfastly dedicated to his calling – equally pragmatic and inspired – and who embodied British engineering innovation in the Victorian era. His extraordinary life saw him rise from a humble working class background in the north of England, playing as a boy near the wooden tram road at the family cottage at Wylam near Newcastle upon Tyne, to become the "Father of the Railways". An inability to read or write before the age of 18 proved no barrier to him making fundamental improvements to the steam engine, revolutionizing transport in making travel by rail a viable option for the first time and ushering in a new era of mass transport for goods and people. It is to his memory and achievements that this book is humbly dedicated.

RECOMMENDATIONS

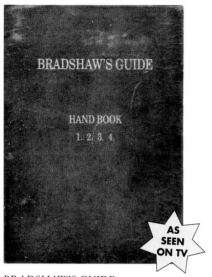

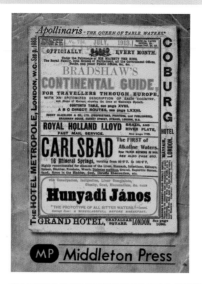

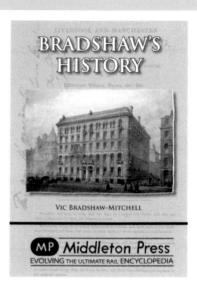

BRADSHAW'S GUIDE:
The 1866 Handbook Reprinted.
ISBN 9781908174055

BRADSHAW'S CONTINENTAL GUIDE:
The 1913 Handbook Reprinted.
ISBN 9781908174246

BRADSHAW'S HISTORY: The compelling
story of the famous George Bradshaw.
ISBN 9781908174185

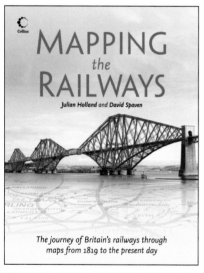

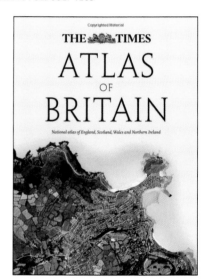

THE TIMES MAPPING THE RAILWAYS:
The journey of Britain's railways through
maps from 1819 to the present day.
ISBN 9780007435999

THE TIMES ATLAS OF LONDON:
Maps the story of the capital from its humble
beginnings to the megacity it is today.
ISBN 9780007434220

THE TIMES ATLAS OF BRITAIN
Perfect for finding out more about
Britain, discovering your county or
just exploring the country.
ISBN 9780007345830

Mapseeker Books –
Armchair Time Travellers Series

Mapseeker Historic Counties Maps

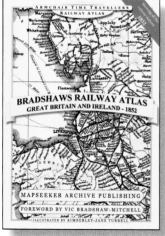

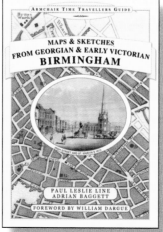

BRADSHAW'S RAILWAY ATLAS OF
GREAT BRITAIN AND IRELAND
Hardcover: ISBN 9781844917914   £29.99
Softcover: ISBN 9781844917907   £19.99

MAPS AND SKETCHES OF GEORGIAN
AND EARLY VICTORIAN BIRMINGHAM
Hardcover: ISBN 9781844918195   £29.99
Softcover: ISBN 9781844918164   £19.99

A COLLECTION OF FOUR
HISTORIC MAPS OF
OXFORDSHIRE
FROM 1611–1836:
ISBN 9781844918140 £19.99

A COLLECTION OF FOUR
HISTORIC MAPS OF
CAMBRIDGESHIRE
FROM 1611–1836:
ISBN 9781844918157 £19.99

A COLLECTION OF FOUR
HISTORIC MAPS OF
BRISTOL
FROM 1851–1903:
ISBN 9781844918171 £19.99